ALSO BY DAVID FRUM

*The Right Man: The Surprise Presidency
of George W. Bush*

*How We Got Here:
The 70's: The Decade That Brought You
Modern Life—for Better or Worse*

*What's Right: The New Conservative Majority
and the Remaking of America*

Dead Right

ALSO BY RICHARD PERLE

Hard Line

AN END
TO EVIL

AN END
TO EVIL

HOW TO WIN THE WAR ON TERROR

David Frum

Richard Perle

RANDOM HOUSE

NEW YORK

Copyright © 2003 by David Frum and Richard Perle

All rights reserved under International and Pan-American Copyright
Conventions. Published in the United States by Random House,
an imprint of The Random House Publishing Group, a division
of Random House, Inc., New York, and simultaneously in Canada by
Random House of Canada Limited, Toronto.

RANDOM HOUSE and colophon are registered trademarks of
Random House, Inc.

Library of Congress Cataloging-in-Publication is available.

ISBN 1-4000-6194-6

Printed in the United States of America on acid-free paper
Random House website address: www.atrandom.com
2 4 6 8 9 7 5 3 1
First Edition

Book design by Victoria Wong

To Florence Rosberg

teacher, reader, friend, grandmother—
and for ninety years an American patriot

—D.F.

To the memory of my friend and
mentor Albert Wohlstetter and the many
dedicated officials and thinkers
he encouraged and inspired

—R.P.

CONTENTS

AN END
TO EVIL

1. WHAT NOW?

These are the times that try men's souls. The summer soldier
and the sunshine patriot will, in this crisis, shrink from the service of their country; but he that stands it now, deserves the
love and thanks of man and woman. Tyranny, like hell, is not
easily conquered; yet we have this consolation with us, that
the harder the conflict, the more glorious the triumph.
— THOMAS PAINE, *The American Crisis,* 1780

W E TOO LIVE in trying times—and thus far our fellow
Americans have passed every test. They have shown
themselves, as President Bush said in his speech in the National Cathedral on September 14, 2001, "generous and kind,
resourceful and brave." They have fought and won two campaigns on the opposite side of the globe, saving millions of
Afghans from famine and the nation of Iraq from tyranny.
They have hunted down terrorists and killers, while respecting the rights of the innocent. And they have uncomplainingly
accepted inconvenience and danger through tiresome years of
lineups at airports, searches at public buildings, and exposure
to further acts of terror.

Now comes the hardest test of all. The war on terror is not over. In many ways, it has barely begun. Al-Qaeda, Hezbollah, and Hamas still plot murder, and money still flows from donors worldwide to finance them. Mullahs preach jihad from the pulpits of mosques from Bengal to Brooklyn. Iran and North Korea are working frantically to develop nuclear weapons. While our enemies plot, our allies dither and carp, and much of our own government remains ominously unready for the fight. We have much to do and scant time in which to do it.

Yet at this dangerous moment many in the American political and media elite are losing their nerve for the fight. Perhaps it is the political cycle: For some Democrats, winning the war has become a less urgent priority than winning the next election. Perhaps it is the media, rediscovering its bias in favor of bad news and infecting the whole country with its own ingrown pessimism. Perhaps it is Congress, resenting the war's cost and coveting the money for its own domestic spending agendas.

Or perhaps it is just fatigue. President Bush warned Americans from the start that the war on terror would be long and difficult and expensive. But in 2001 those warnings were just words. Today they are realities. And while the American people have shouldered those realities magnificently, America's leaders too often seem to flinch from them. Every difficulty, every casualty, every reverse seems to throw Washington, D.C., into a panic—as if there had ever been a war without difficulties, without casualties, without reverses. In the war on terror, the United States has as yet suffered no defeats, except of course for 9/11 itself. But defeats may well occur, for they too are part of war, and we shudder to think how some of our leaders in their current mood will respond.

We can feel the will to win ebbing in Washington; we sense the reversion to the bad old habits of complacency and denial.

Throughout the 1990s, thousands of terrorists received training in the al-Qaeda camps of Afghanistan—and our government passively monitored the situation. Terrorists attacked and murdered Americans in East Africa, in Yemen, in Saudi Arabia—and America responded to these acts of war as if they were ordinary crimes. Iraq flagrantly violated the terms of its 1991 armistice—and our government from time to time fired a cruise missile into Baghdad but otherwise did little. Iran defied the Monroe Doctrine and sponsored murder in our own hemisphere, killing eighty-six people and wounding some three hundred at a Jewish Community Center in Buenos Aires—and our government did worse than nothing: It opened negotiations with the murderers. Mullahs and imams incited violence and slaughter against Christians and Jews—and our government failed to acknowledge that anything important was occurring.

September 11 is supposed to have changed all that. Since the attacks on the World Trade Center and the Pentagon, terrorism has become the first priority of our government. Or so it is said—but is it true? The forces and the people who lulled the United States into complacency in the 1990s remain potent today, and in the wake of the victories in Afghanistan and Iraq, they are exerting themselves ever more boldly.

With a few stalwart exceptions, such as Senator Joe Lieberman, the administration's Democratic opponents seem ready to give up the fight altogether. They want to give up on Iraq. They denounce the Patriot Act. They condemn President Bush's policies (in the words of Richard Gephardt) as a "miserable failure." Traveling to France in October 2003 to criticize her country, former secretary of state Madeleine Albright declared, "Bush and the people under him have a foreign policy that is not good for America, not good for the world." But as to what to do instead, they say nothing, leaving the impression that they wish to do nothing.

Nor is it only the president's political opponents who seem bereft of ideas. At the State Department, there is constant pressure to return to business as usual, beginning by placating offended allies and returning to the exaggerated multilateral conceit of the Clinton administration. Generals, diplomats, and lawmakers who retired and now work for the Saudi government or Saudi companies huff and puff at the damage the war on terror is doing to the U.S.-Saudi relationship. Members of Congress complain about the cost of fighting terror. On television, respected commentators intone about quagmires and overstretch. Leading journalists deplore Muslim and European anti-Americanism in a way that implies *we* are its cause.

If you ask them, many of these respectable characters will insist that they remain keen to wage war on terrorism. But press them a little, and it quickly becomes clear that they define "terror" very narrowly. They are eager to arrest the misfits and thugs who plant bombs and carry guns. But as for the larger networks that recruit the misfits and thugs, as for the wealthy donors who pay the terrorists' bills, as for the governments that give terrorists aid and sanctuary, as for the larger culture of incitement and hatred that justifies and supports terror: All of that they wish to leave alone. As the inevitable disappointments and difficulties of war accumulate, as weariness with war's costs and rigors spreads, as memories of 9/11 fade, the advocates of a weaker line against terror have pressed their timid case. Like rust and mildew, they make the most progress when they receive the least attention, for their desired policy coincides with the natural predilections of government.

President Bush's war on terror jerked our national security bureaucracy out of its comfortable routines. He demanded that the military fight new wars in new ways. He demanded that our intelligence services second-guess their familiar assumptions. He demanded that the State Department speak firmly and forcefully to those who claim to be our friends. He demanded that our public diplomacy make the case for America without apology. He demanded fresh thought and strong measures and clear language—none of which comes naturally to any part of the vast bureaucracy that Americans employ to protect the nation.

All of this departure from the ordinary has generated resentment and resistance. The resisters are supported by the heavy weight of inertia, by every governmental instinct toward regularity and predictability and caution, by the bureaucracy's profound aversion to innovation, controversy, and confrontation. And let us not forget that, for all the bravery of our soldiers, our military is a bureaucracy, too: It didn't like being told that cavalry had to make way for the tank, and the battleship for the aircraft carrier; it doesn't like it any better when contemporary modernizers tell it that artillery must give way to the smart missile or that conventional tactics must be reinvented for a new era. Really, it's no wonder that those few policy makers who have urged a strong policy against terror have been called a "cabal." To the enormous majority in any government who wish to continue to do things as they have always been done, the tiny minority that dares propose anything new will always look like a presumptuous, unrealistic, intriguing faction.

Taken all in all, it could well be said that we have reached the crisis point in the war on terror. The momentum of our victories has flagged. The way forward has become uncertain and the challenges ahead of us more complex. The ranks of the faint hearts are growing, and their voices are echoing ever more loudly in our media and our politics.

Yet tomorrow could be the day that an explosive packed with radioactive material detonates in Los Angeles or that nerve gas is unleashed inside a tunnel under the Hudson River or that a terrible new disease breaks out in the United Kingdom. If the people responsible for the 9/11 attack could have killed thirty thousand Americans or three hundred thousand or three million, they would have done so. The terrorists are cruel, but they are not aimless. Their actions have a purpose. They are trying to rally the Muslim world to jihad against the planet's only superpower and the principal and most visible obstacle to their ambitions. They commit terror to persuade their potential followers that their cause is not hopeless, that jihad can destroy American power. Random killings—shootings in shopping malls, bombs in trash cans—may be emotionally satisfying to the terrorists, but they are strategically useless: Two kids at Columbine did as much, and the Republic did not totter. Only truly spectacular acts of mass murder provides the propaganda the terrorists' cause requires. They will try again—they have to.

Throughout the war, the advocates of a strong policy against terror have had one great advantage over those who prefer the weaker line: We have offered concrete recommendations equal to the seriousness of the threat, and the softliners have not, because we have wanted to fight, and they have not. For us, terrorism remains the great evil of our time, and the war against this evil, our generation's great cause. We do not believe that Americans are fighting this evil to minimize it or to manage it. We believe they are fighting to win—to end this evil before it kills again and on a genocidal scale. There is no middle way for Americans: It is victory or holocaust. This book is a manual for victory.

2. END OF THE BEGINNING

P ESSIMISM AND DEFEATISM have provided the sound track to the war on terrorism from the beginning, first in Afghanistan, then in Iraq. Remember the "dreaded Afghan winter"? Remember how the Iraq war was "bogging down" when allied forces paused for two days to wait out a sandstorm? In Afghanistan, U.S. troops astonished the world with a whole new kind of war on land and in the air. In Iraq, U.S. forces overthrew Saddam Hussein's entire regime with half the troops and in half the time it took merely to shove Saddam out of Kuwait in 1991.* It did not matter: The gloomsayers were unembarrassable. Having been proven wrong when they predicted the United States would sink into a forlorn quagmire in Iraq, they reappeared days later to insist that while military victory had been assured from the beginning, the United States was now losing the peace: There was looting throughout the country; the national museum had supposedly been sacked;

---

* Specifically: 250,000 U.S. and U.K. forces in 2003 vs. 660,000 coalition forces in 1991; forty-eight vs. twenty-six days of air and ground operations. Max Boot, "The New American Way of War," *Foreign Affairs* (July–August 2003): 41–58, at p. 43.

hospitals had been stripped bare by thieves; power was blacked out; and sewage was running into the Euphrates.

Now the pessimists are quivering because the remnants of the Baath Party have launched a guerrilla war against the allied forces in Iraq. These guerrillas are former secret policemen and informers, the regime's specially recruited enforcers, murderers, torturers, and rapists. They are men with nowhere to go. If they are found, they will be tried for their crimes, unless the families of their victims kill them first. The surviving leaders of the regime, hidden by one another, have money. It is not hard for them to recruit these desperate characters into paramilitary units and terrorist cells—what other future do they have? But it is wrong to describe these paid killers as a "national resistance," as some even normally sensible people have sometimes done. For a dozen years after Appomattox, former Confederate soldiers terrorized their neighbors, robbed trains, and killed Union soldiers. Was the Ku Klux Klan a "national resistance"? Was Jesse James?

The aftermath of war is always messy and often bloody. In the six months after the liberation of Paris in 1944, the French killed upward of ten thousand accused collaborators. A dozen years after the fall of communism, electricity and water sputter unreliably in much of the former Soviet Union. A Swedish journalist who visited Germany one and a half years after the end of World War II observed that

the electricity is still out. People are "bitter, disillusioned and hopeless." They express fury at the Allies, especially the English, whom they believe to be "sabotaging renewal." Many argue that things are worse than under the old dictatorship. On the streets, foreign correspondents interview barefoot orphans, who clamour for an American visa. Above all, there looms the profound hypocrisy of the occupation itself, and its "attempt to eradicate militarism by means of a military regime." *

Post-Saddam Iraq has emerged from more than three decades of totalitarian rule and mass murder, from more than a decade of economic sanctions and systematic corruption, and finally from a month of deadly accurate bombing. Should anyone have been surprised that it took the United States a few weeks to get the lights working?

Yet a good many people who ought to have known better *did* claim to be surprised. And they have claimed more than that. They have claimed that the Iraq campaign somehow detracted from the overall war against terror—and that Saddam's success in concealing his weapons of mass destruction program somehow proves that he should have been left in power to build those weapons. These critics complained that President Bush weakened the case for war by offering too many different justifications for it. It never seemed to bother them that they had more than one reason for doing nothing— and that unlike the president's, their reasons contradicted one another:

* Amity Shlaes, "Iraqi Echoes of Postwar Germany," *Financial Times*, July 28, 2003, p. 18. Shlaes is paraphrasing and quoting the Swedish journalist Stig Dagerman, whose *German Autumn* was originally published in 1947.

- Opponents of the Iraq war like German foreign minister Joschka Fischer protested that they were "not convinced" that Saddam possessed weapons of mass destruction at all.[*] Meanwhile, former national security adviser Brent Scowcroft warned that if attacked, Saddam would retaliate with weapons of mass murder "unleashing an Armageddon in the Middle East."[†]

- Opponents of the war insisted that Saddam had no connections with terrorism. Then they fretted, in the words of Senator Edward M. Kennedy, that if the United States attempted to overthrow Saddam, the United States could instead "precipitate the very threat that we are intent on preventing—weapons of mass destruction in the hands of terrorists."[‡]

- Like General Barry McCaffrey, they predicted a military disaster in which the United States could potentially suffer, "bluntly, a couple to 3,000 casualties."[§] And then they accused the United States of picking on a country too weak to pose a threat.

- They insisted that action against Iran and North Korea should take priority over the defeat of Saddam Hussein's

---

[*] news.bbc.co.uk/2/hi/europe/2740777.stm.

[†] *The Wall Street Journal*, August 15, 2002, p. A12.

[‡] "Eliminating the Threat: The Right Course of Action for Disarming Iraq, Combating Terrorism, Protecting the Homeland, and Stabilizing the Middle East," remarks at the School of Advanced International Studies," September 27, 2002, www.kennedy/senate/gov.

[§] Rory McCarthy and Julian Borger, "Battle for Baghdad Begins," *The Guardian*, March 25, 2003, www.guardian.co.uk/Iraq/Story/0,2763,921387,00.html.

regime. Now that Saddam's regime has been defeated and the Bush administration stands ready to follow their advice about Iran and North Korea, their enthusiasm for action against those other rogue regimes has suddenly withered away.

- They swore that nobody deplored Saddam's crimes more than they. As House minority leader Nancy Pelosi said in March 2003, "Those who [suggest] that there is any sympathy for Saddam Hussein in the world do a grave disservice to the debate." Yet as U.S. forces uncovered what may prove to be more than a hundred mass graves containing upwards of three hundred thousand victims, they showed virtually zero interest.

- They were shocked and offended whenever anyone questioned their patriotism or good faith. And since the war ended, they have followed the example of former vice president Gore and accused President Bush and Prime Minister Tony Blair of "bending our entire national security policy to fit their political designs."*

---

* *This Week with George Stephanopoulos*, December 8, 2002. It should be noted that Gore prefaced his accusation by piously disclaiming any intention to accuse anybody. Read in full, however, Gore's true meaning is manifest:

> Well, again, you know, the reason I don't want to accuse them of bending our entire national security policy to fit their political designs is it's such a serious charge, you don't know what's inside their hearts. The very fact that they've left that out there for people to suspect is not good for our country, and, and of course, you know we had this high-level resignation in the White House from John DiIulio, who told one of the nation's magazines that all of the decisions in the White House now are driven by political motivations.

So let's go back to the beginning, to where we were after 9/11 and to the reasons that guided President Bush to his decision to pursue the war on terror to the ancient battlefields of Mesopotamia.

"Weakness is provocative": That's one of Donald Rumsfeld's famous rules, and a decade of weakness in the Middle East had proved Rumsfeld right.

In 1991, President George H. W. Bush called on the people of Iraq to rise up against Saddam Hussein. In Shiite southern Iraq, the people did as the president asked—and they were mowed down in the thousands by the Republican Guard units we had allowed to escape from Desert Storm and by the helicopter gunships General Norman Schwarzkopf had foolishly permitted Saddam to fly. The United States could have grounded those helicopters. We could have supplied weapons to the Iraqi people. We could have cut roads and communications between the rebellion in southern Iraq and Saddam's armed forces in the north. We could have warned that commanders who massacred civilians would be held accountable for their crimes—and we could have moved our forces forward a few miles deeper into Iraq to give that warning extra meaning.

We did none of those things. The rebellion was crushed as we stood by. Nobody should have been surprised that when we returned to Iraq a dozen years later, many Iraqis had not forgotten—or forgiven.

The first Bush administration had its reasons for holding back in 1991. When it had called for an uprising, it had something very different in mind: a coup in Baghdad by one of Saddam's Sunni henchmen. This was and remained the remedy for Saddam recommended by the Central Intelligence Agency. The CIA contended that the mass uprising in the south might bring to power Shiite extremists who would then tilt toward Shiite Iran. The Agency feared that a Shiite victory in Iraq might spread troublesome ideas among the oppressed Shiites of our client Saudi Arabia. The CIA's hesitations were seconded by Secretary of State James Baker and National Security Adviser Brent Scowcroft, who wanted no responsibility for governing a post-Saddam Iraq, and by Colin Powell, then chairman of the Joint Chiefs of Staff, who believed that expelling Saddam from Kuwait was more than enough heavy lifting for the armed forces of the United States. And the president? He believed Saddam was finished anyway after the catastrophic defeat inflicted by the coalition—there was no need for the United States to do anything more. (Colin Powell still believed it ten years later. At the famous Camp David meetings on September 15 and 16, 2001, Powell sought to end any discussion of Iraq by saying curtly, "But we won.")

These calculations, sophisticated, subtle, and wrong, persuaded the first President Bush in 1991. But what Iraqis and others in the Middle East saw was Saddam's tanks crushing American-backed insurgents. Saddam had survived; therefore we had lost. And over the next eight years the people of the region would see us lose again and again. So bewildered were the region's people by America's failure to support the 1991 uprising that the idea took hold that the United States actually wanted Saddam to remain in power. Confusion about the true desires of the United States made it almost impossible to rally Saddam's neighbors against his regime—and in 2003 the memory of this confusion aided the Baathist remnants, who started a whispering campaign warning Iraqis to be careful not to condemn Saddam, for the Americans themselves would soon restore the Baathists to power.

In April 1993, Saddam Hussein plotted to assassinate former president George H. W. Bush during a visit to Kuwait.* The new Clinton administration responded to this extreme provocation by firing cruise missiles into the headquarters of Saddam's secret police—at midnight, when the torturers and murderers who worked there had gone home and nobody but hapless janitors could be expected to be found on the premises. Lest even this feeble retaliation seem too aggressive, a Clinton spokesman actually announced that the strike had been timed to minimize Iraqi casualties.

In 1995 and 1996, the Clinton administration gave its support to an anti-Saddam military coup, disregarding warnings from the Iraqi resistance that the coup had been compromised. In July 1996, Saddam's agents arrested more than two hundred senior officers and executed eighty of them. The Iraqis even captured the communications equipment the CIA had provided the plotters, a fact that was learned when the CIA station at Amman, Jordan, picked up an incoming call—

---

* Future First Lady Laura Bush accompanied the former president and might well have become a casualty herself.

and heard the cackles of Saddam's killers on the other end of the line.

A month after the botched coup, Saddam struck at the main Iraqi resistance movement, the Iraqi National Congress, by invading the INC's bases in the U.S.-guaranteed Kurdish safe haven in northern Iraq. The Clinton administration did nothing to help the Kurds it had promised to protect: Instead it fired off another round of cruise missiles at targets in Baghdad and the south.

In 1998, Saddam Hussein at last succeeded in forcing the United Nations weapons inspectors to leave Iraq. Although Saddam had agreed to inspections as a condition of peace at the end of the Gulf War, he never cooperated with them. In June 1991, Iraqi troops fired at the very first inspection mission, when the inspectors approached too close to an Iraqi nuclear site. For the next seven years, Saddam harassed, wiretapped, infiltrated, and threatened the inspectors. By 1998, he had made their work so difficult and futile that they withdrew from the country. President Clinton had described the work of the inspectors as "vital" to American national security. But when this supposedly vital interest was jeopardized, Clinton merely ordered yet another barrage of air strikes. These December 1998 strikes, code-named Operation Desert Fox, have to be reckoned as one of Saddam's greatest triumphs. Saddam shrugged them off, and Clinton gave up. Saddam had taken the measure of the American administration he faced. At the price of a few smashed-up buildings, Saddam escaped inspections seemingly forever.

"When people see a strong horse and a weak horse, by nature, they will like the strong horse." Whether or not this observation of Osama bin Laden's is universally true, it certainly applies in much of the Arab world—and two American administrations had together persuaded many in that world that Saddam Hussein was a stronger horse than the United States.

And getting stronger. After ridding himself of the UN arms inspectors, Saddam next sought to escape the economic sanctions and arms embargo the UN had imposed on him back in 1990. For eight years, these sanctions had restricted Iraq's ability to sell oil, and though they were circumvented through a variety of schemes and dodges, they operated well enough to squeeze Saddam's ability to purchase costly weapons. But by 1998, the sanctions regime too was falling apart. Iraq was smuggling billions of dollars' worth of oil out of the country, much of it through Syria and Iran. And Saddam was acquiring technologies like secure fiber-optic communications networks, which served important military purposes but could be described as "nonmilitary" because they could also be used by civilian customers, if any had existed in impoverished, state-controlled Iraq.

Propaganda in the Arab world and elsewhere successfully misrepresented the sanctions as the cause of death and suffering in Iraq. In his famous fatwa of February 1998, Osama bin Laden cited sanctions as one of his three justifications for waging holy war against Jews and "crusaders": "Despite the great devastation inflicted on the Iraqi people by the crusader-Zionist alliance, and despite the huge number of those killed, which has exceeded one million . . . despite all this, the Americans are once again trying to repeat the horrific massacres, as though they are not content with the protracted blockade imposed after the ferocious war or the fragmentation and devastation."

The UN-administered oil-for-food program could have delivered all essential food, medicine, and other necessities to the people of Iraq. But it could not do so without the cooperation of the Iraqi government, and Saddam personally ensured that his people's needs went unmet in order to lend credence to his regime's propaganda. On the very day that Iraq was liberated, $13 billion in oil-for-food funds sat unexpended in the program's escrow account in Paris. Saddam perverted the oil-for-food program to his own benefit. There is good reason to believe that many of the transactions that the UN approved—transactions that were labeled as purchases of cooking oil, or grain, or hospital equipment—were fraudulent in whole or in part and that billions of dollars from them were redirected or stolen. The program could more accurately have been called oil-for-palaces. It must be said, however, that Saddam could never have gotten away with his thefts without the tacit acquiescence of the UN itself. The UN helped itself to a 1.5 percent commission on all the money that flowed through the secretive program. This rake-off earned the UN many hundreds of millions of dollars a year—a valuable income source to an organization whose own accounting is anything but a model of transparency. Oil-for-food, in other words, was an institutionalized conflict of interest, and it swiftly degenerated into a corrupt deal that benefited Saddam's elite, the UN bureaucracy, and the program's French bankers—and only last and least the people of Iraq.

Osama bin Laden's one million casualty figure was bogus. Nevertheless, the sufferings of the people of Iraq were very real. Real too were the economic opportunities that beckoned to Saddam's trading partners if the sanctions should be dropped. Pressure to abandon sanctions mounted on the Clinton administration. The governments of France and Russia demanded that sanctions be scrapped. So did the Arab and third world lobbies at the UN. So too did a gathering international protest movement. Former Australian prime minister Malcolm Fraser signed a petition calling for the immediate abolition of Iraq sanctions. U.S. senator Patty Murray, U.S. representative Tom Campbell, two United Nations humanitarian coordinators for Iraq, and the official spokesman for the Vatican—among many others—denounced sanctions as well.

The Clinton administration, characteristically, wavered. On the one hand, the administration lacked the strength of character to resist these pressures. On the other, sanctions were all that remained of the administration's crumbling claim to have "contained" Saddam. ("He's in a box" was the phrase favored by Secretary of State Madeleine Albright and National Security Adviser Sandy Berger.) So, again characteristically, the Clintonites began looking for some form of words that would allow them to surrender while pretending to themselves and to others that they had held firm. They began looking for ways to relax the sanctions without formally abrogating them.

The 2000 election intervened before the Clinton administration could put its new policy in place. The incoming Bush administration inherited—and Secretary of State Colin Powell quickly adopted—the Clinton plan, now renamed "smart sanctions." But France (Iraq's largest trading partner) and Russia (Iraq's largest creditor) used their power in the Security Council to defeat "smart sanctions." Rather than mitigate the sanctions regime, France and Russia preferred to leave the existing sanctions in place until they collapsed altogether.

Thus, by the summer of 2001, we were confronting an Iraq that stood a good chance of escaping the controls that had been placed on it in 1990 and 1991. The inspectors were gone. Maintaining the sanctions required a new UN vote every six months. We knew that the UN inspectors had found and destroyed only some of the weapons that Iraq itself had declared back in 1991. We knew that Iraq had almost certainly built additional weapons, weapons components, and weapons materials in the 1990s. We knew that Iraq retained the skills and knowledge to build biological and nuclear weapons. We knew that Saddam Hussein desperately wanted these weapons. We knew that it was only a matter of time before he would regain the resources to acquire them.

And we knew one thing more: We knew that our own best

information had consistently underestimated the danger from Iraq. In the 1980s, the national security agencies and the intelligence community concluded that the Israeli strike that destroyed Iraq's French-made Osirak nuclear reactor just before it could be loaded with nuclear fuel had set back the Iraqi bomb program for a generation or longer. But when we got hold of the Iraqi defense records after the Gulf War in 1991, we discovered that the Iraqis had immediately started work on a separate, clandestine nuclear weapons program of their own.

A footnote to history: The man who headed the International Atomic Energy Agency (IAEA) in 1990 was Hans Blix, the Swedish bureaucrat who would lead the UN inspection mission to Iraq in 2002–2003. Saddam's past success in carrying out a secret nuclear program under Blix's nose may explain why Saddam insisted (through his UN mouthpieces France and Russia) that Blix be chosen in place of more effective inspectors, such as Australia's Richard Butler, Sweden's Rolf Ekeus, or America's David Kay.

Likewise, our intelligence services could find no evidence to contradict the Iraqis when they told us after Desert Storm that they had halted their biological weapons program—until Saddam Hussein's son-in-law Hussein Kamel defected in 1995, and we learned of Iraq's continuing attempts to weaponize anthrax, plague, botulism, and smallpox.

So when we caught the Iraqis in the late 1990s importing the raw materials for chemical weapons, and other parts and components that could be necessary to the making of a nuclear bomb, it seemed like basic common sense to assume the worst. Our easygoing intelligence analysts had got Saddam wrong again and again. Now we had to consider: Where would Saddam be in 2004, 2005, and 2006? Would he obtain nuclear material from North Korea or from the Russian mafia? To what projects would he assign his team of nuclear experts? Would he develop ballistic missiles? Bioweapons? How would he use his new weapons if he got them? Directly against us? Indirectly through terrorism? Would he try again to conquer Kuwait to seize its oil wealth—and this time learn from his 1990 mistake and threaten mass casualties in the United States if we intervened to stop him? Or would he seek glory in the Arab world by attacking Israel, possibly triggering a nuclear confrontation?

The failure to find stockpiles of weapons of mass destruction has led some Bush (and Blair) administration critics to charge that the president and prime minister deliberately "hyped" or "sexed up" or otherwise exaggerated the danger posed by Saddam Hussein in order to justify a war to remove his regime. Others have demanded investigations into the intelligence basis for the two leaders' conclusion that it would have been risky and imprudent to leave Saddam in place.

The critics' emphasis on *stockpiles* of chemical or biological weapons as the central issue seems to us seriously misplaced. As David Kay has reported, there is overwhelming evidence that Saddam had extensive chemical and biological weapons *programs,* that he went to great lengths to conceal from inspectors a range of activity—all in violation of numerous U.N. resolutions—that would have enabled him to produce such weapons in the future, that facilities were built and maintained for that purpose, that the necessary skilled manpower had been secretly and deceptively organized, and that this broad effort included work on unmanned aircraft and missiles with ranges sufficient to attack well beyond Iraqi territory. Even in the absence of stockpiles of weapons Saddam was known to have created, the threat from his programs was undeniable.

In these matters, presidents and prime ministers must make judgments based on the best available evidence, and they must weigh that evidence carefully, always mindful of the consequences of acting under conditions of uncertainty. A failure to act on the available intelligence by taking the risk that Saddam did not possess weapons of mass destruction and therefore leaving him in place could have catastrophic consequences. Action to remove him, even though the evidence of his weapons of mass destruction was uncertain, would involve the dangers and costs of war, but these would entail far less risk, far less danger, than discovering too late that he did indeed have the chemical and biological weapons he was known to have produced.

President Bush had to ask himself: "If I remove Saddam and learn later that he did not have weapons of mass destruction after all, how would that compare to leaving him in place—and learning only after he used them, or enabled terrorists to use them, that he *did* in fact possess the chemical and biological weapons that all Western intelligence organizations as well as United Nations inspectors believed him to have hidden away?" Where intelligence is uncertain, prudent leaders will inevitably minimize risk by erring on the side of the worst plausible assumption. And rightly so.

Saddam Hussein's ambitions were dangerous enough before 9/11; afterward, they had to be regarded as a clear and present danger to the United States. The war on terror was certain to create all kinds of new opportunities for Saddam to exploit. He published magazine editions cheering the destruction of the World Trade Center: Bin Laden had struck home. Saddam expected to share in his success.

The threat presented by Saddam was global, for his mischief making limited our options for dealing with other regional threats, such as Iran or North Korea. In the spring and summer of 1994, North Korea triggered an international crisis by threatening to remove plutonium from its nuclear reactor at Yongbyon and process it into nuclear weapons. In the fall of that same year, while the Clinton administration was trying to decide what to do about North Korea, Saddam moved troops and tanks southward to the Kuwait border. President Clinton issued a stern statement: "Saddam Hussein," he said, "should be under no illusions; the United States is not otherwise occupied. . . ." But the United States was occupied enough. The Clinton administration was reluctant to confront two large foreign crises at the same time. In October 1994, the United States rushed troops to Kuwait to deter Saddam—but in that very same month it also signed a nuclear agreement with North Korea that rewarded the North Koreans with hundreds of millions of dollars for fuel and food. The agreement even committed the United States to build the North Koreans two American-style nuclear reactors. The North Koreans, of course, promptly reneged on the deal and commenced a separate, secret uranium enrichment program. From this painful experience, the incoming George W. Bush administration drew the conclusion that if it wished ever to be able to deal forcefully with North Korea or anybody else, it had better eliminate Saddam first.

Even if Saddam Hussein refrained from waging or threatening war on us and our allies, his looming triumph over the inspectors and the sanctions would have emboldened and inspired terrorists around the world. Suicide bombers do not join a terrorist movement in order to die a futile death. Killers need hope, too. The disinclination of the Clinton administration to respond forcefully to the escalating terror attacks of the 1990s encouraged the terrorists to plan the spectacular attacks of 9/11. Had 9/11 been followed by a resurgence of Saddam's power, the United States would have broadcast to the world an even more lethal message: The Americans are weakening. The future belongs to America's enemies.

So we had to strike back and hard after 9/11, to prove that terrorism was *not* winning. Had we fought only in Afghanistan and then stopped, we would have conveyed the message that we were willing to accept the easy missions in the war on terror, but not the hard ones. We would have projected trepidation and uncertainty when we needed more than ever to show confidence and strength. For all those reasons, we had to continue from Afghanistan on to Iraq.

"O mujahideen brothers in Iraq," said a tape purportedly recorded by Osama bin Laden and broadcast in February 2003, "do not be afraid of what the United States is propagating in terms of their lies about their power and their smart, laser-guided missiles." By clutching Saddam Hussein's regime by the throat and throwing it against the wall, the United States demonstrated that bin Laden's boasts were false—that the United States was overwhelmingly strong, that the terrorists' hopes of somehow toppling the American government were delusions, and that attacks upon the United States would bring nothing but destruction upon the attackers.

Many in the Arab and Muslim world expected that Saddam would bloody the coalition forces arrayed against him. Some in Europe seem to have hoped so, too. When asked at a press conference in London whether he wished for the United States to win in Iraq, French foreign minister Dominique de Villepin declined to answer. In the event, Saddam's armies collapsed in less than three weeks, and Saddam himself fled for safety. The historian Niall Ferguson has aptly called the overthrow of Saddam "the mother of all wake-up calls." "When five Arab leaders met Mr. Bush on [June 3, 2003]," Ferguson observed, "they pledged, with manifest penitence, that they would henceforth actively fight 'the culture of extremism and violence.' Not just al Qaeda: Hamas and Hezbollah too."* Saddam's rule had been justified by one claim: his strength. He may have been a homicidal tyrant, but

* Niall Ferguson, "The 'E' Word," *The Wall Street Journal,* June 6, 2003, p. A10.

in the eyes of many of those Arab and Muslim people who did not themselves have to live in Iraq, every crime was excused by Saddam's stature as the one Arab who seemed to inspire genuine fear in the West. In the words of Rami Khouri, the influential editor of the *Jordan Times:* "Saddam Hussein's fearlessness in standing up to our enemies . . . appeals to the new spirit of the Arab world—a spirit that says we'd rather die on our feet than live groveling on the ground."* Khouri is generally regarded as an Arab moderate.

But what if Saddam's cruelty had accomplished nothing, had contributed in no way to Arab strength and dignity? What then? Might Arab intellectuals *then* speak out against his crimes? Indeed, that is exactly what has happened since the overthrow of Saddam's regime.

"We all saw the film of the execution and murder [of victims by] blowing them up by remote control with explosives stuffed into their pockets," wrote Rajah al-Khuri in the Lebanese newspaper *al-Nahar* on May 20, 2003, referring to a video broadcast of some of Saddam's atrocities. "Later, we saw the [executioners] applauding as the victims flew into the air, their limbs torn apart and covered with dust. We felt something precious within our human dignity blown up [with these sights]. . . . We felt that we, in some way or another, shared partly in the guilt, because murderers who came from our Arab world perpetrated this kind of savageness.

"[These murderers] had sold [the Arab world] the slogans

---

* Quoted in Kanan Makiya, *Cruelty and Silence* (Norton, 1993), p. 244.

of nationalism and progressiveness while riding on the back of the ideology of Arabism, which they prostituted. . . . This barbarism, unprecedented in human history, was committed by Arab hands, by hands that found such delight in death and murder that the death squads would send the heads of the victims to Saddam Hussein's two sons in cardboard boxes. . . .

"These plastic bags in the mass graves contained bulletriddled skulls, [bodies] wrapped in rags, [tied] in ropes, [or] dressed in worn pieces of clothing. . . . Ropes still tied a mother's bones to her infant's and a father's to his son's. . . ."*

As Arab anger gathered against the horrors of Saddam's rule, that anger extended next to Saddam's apologists.

"Many Arabs sinned . . . against the Iraqi people when they stood by its executioners," charged the journalist Ahmed al-Rab'i in a London Arabic newspaper, "when they underestimated the savagery with which the [Iraqi] regime treated its own people, when they opened up their media to anyone defending this ghoulish regime, and when they refused to treat others' opinions tolerantly. It is about time that some of them stand, with a minimum of self-respect, and apologize to the Iraqis."†

Finally, and most boldly, came the insight that the horror of Iraq indicted not merely Saddam's tyranny and its supporters, but all Arab tyrannies and all of their supporters.

"While the late [Baathist] regime slaughtered its own

* www.memri.org/bin/latestnews.cgi?ID=SD51903#_edn3.
† Ibid.

people for decades," observed the writer Salem Mashkur also in *al-Nahar*, "all these 'Jihad warriors' and the various Arab 'fighters,' secular and religious, held their tongues. Some even welcomed this slaughter; others justified their silence [by claiming] it was a foreign conspiracy . . . !

"All these arguments [reflect] the . . . official and general Arab discourse: the negligible nothingness of the individual, and disparagement of his liberties, dignity, and even his bones in the mass graves. . . ."*

BY TOPPLING Saddam Hussein, we achieved at least seven great objectives.

1. We put an end to the threat from whatever weapons of mass destruction Saddam actually possessed as of 2003— and, far more important, from those weapons he *would* have possessed had he been left in place.

2. We won a great victory over terrorism by eliminating a Middle Eastern regime that has for thirty years been one of the leading sponsors of terrorism in the region. When Saddam reached out to Osama bin Laden in the early 1990s, he was continuing a tradition that extended back to the days when Iraqi intelligence cooperated with Eastern bloc intelligence services to provide false passports, sanctuary, and instructions in murder to Abu Nidal and Black September.

* Ibid.

3. We denied our enemies in the Middle East the huge victory *they* would have won had Saddam been able to claim that he had survived and triumphed over us.

4. We have learned valuable lessons about how to fight wars in the region and how to rebuild afterward. Nobody will pretend that mistakes were not made in the Iraqi campaign and the subsequent occupation. But we have learned from those mistakes, and they will not be repeated. The United States will continue to become more and more capable and effective in the fight against terror.

5. We gave other potential enemies a vivid and compelling demonstration of America's ability to win swift and total victory over significant enemy forces with minimal U.S. casualties. The overwhelming American victory in the battle of Baghdad surely stamped a powerful impression upon the minds of the rulers of Teheran and Pyongyang.

6. We aided the forces of democracy throughout the region by demonstrating that even the most fearsome local dictatorships are far more fragile than they look.

7. We eliminated the Arab world's cruelest and most tyrannical ruler. We liberated an entire nation, opening the way to a humane, decent civil society in Iraq—and to reform of the ideological and moral climate of the whole Middle East.

These are great accomplishments—yet according to the war's many critics, they are still not enough. Opponents of the Bush administration in Congress and the press sometimes suggest that it was overcautious and unnecessary to worry today about Saddam's weapons of tomorrow. The threat, they say, wasn't "imminent." It was never quite clear how "imminent" would have been imminent enough to suit these critics. Should we have waited until one month before Saddam got a nuclear bomb or weaponized smallpox? One week? Until the stuff actually rolled out of the lab? Until we knew he was preparing to use it? American intelligence is not the all-knowing, all-seeing spy service of the movies: "No need to strike yet, Mr. President, our agents tell us that we have ninety-seven days and thirteen hours before Iraq's new superviruses become usable. . . ." The intelligence services are very human, very imperfect institutions. If we wait to protect ourselves until the CIA determines that it is five minutes to midnight, we will run the ugly risk of discovering that we have waited too long. Certainly we waited too long in the case of Osama bin Laden. We threw away many opportunities to finish him off. In 1996, when bin Laden was expelled from Sudan, the Clinton administration actually concluded that it did not want to take custody of him. It feared it could not convict him in an American criminal court, and it could not think of any way to deal with him *other* than a criminal trial. Today, it is hard to understand this lack of urgency. But if President Bush's critics are correct, President Clinton did exactly the right thing in 1996. The threat from bin Laden was not then "imminent": It would be two whole years before bin Laden's men blew up the embassies in East Africa and five before they killed three thousand people in New York, Washington, and Pennsylvania.

As the bin Laden episode proves, the responsible thing to do when confronted by a foreign threat is to act when we *can,* and the earlier the better. Everything we did after 9/11 to destroy the Taliban regime in Afghanistan and the bin Laden terrorist organization could have been done before 9/11, with two important differences: Three thousand of our citizens might be alive today, and we might well have surprised much of the al-Qaeda network in Afghanistan. Instead, we allowed al-Qaeda to strike first, condemning ourselves to chase its leaders from one prepared hiding place to the next, all around the world.

Even if we could predict dangers more accurately than we can, what benefit do we gain from waiting for a threat to become *more* imminent? Why let an enemy grow stronger unhindered? By waiting until the last minute, we forfeit the initiative. We cast away the opportunity to act at a time and place of our choosing and gamble our security on future circumstances that may or may not be favorable to us. Quite frequently, the real motive of those who advocate delay is the hope that if we postpone action, somehow the threat will disappear on its own. This isn't policy. It's fantasy.

Iraq was a test of American seriousness about the war on terror. It tested whether we truly intended to wage war against our enemies—or whether we would revert to the pinprick tactics of the past. It tested whether we would open our eyes to the danger of Middle Eastern radicalism of all varieties—or whether we would continue to shut our eyes and wish our problems away. It tested whether those flags we flew in the autumn of 2001 attested to our resolve—or merely to a passing flutter of emotion.

Critics of the Iraq war insist that the United States ought to have concentrated all its efforts on al-Qaeda. Well, the Bush administration has acted against al-Qaeda, and it has succeeded. In the two years after 9/11, some two-thirds of the known leadership of al-Qaeda were captured or killed. Khalid Shaikh Mohammed, the planner of the 9/11 attacks, is an American prisoner. So is Abu Anas Liby, who masterminded the 1998 East African embassy bombings. So too is Abu Zubayda, chief administrator of al-Qaeda's Afghan training camps. Information from these men and from other sources has thwarted terrorist operations from Paris to Singapore. That is a triumphant record of success in national self-defense.

The implicit argument of those who opposed the Iraq campaign was that the United States should have stopped after Afghanistan, because going further was too hazardous, too likely to offend Middle Eastern opinion. This is the same fear-haunted counsel that guided the policy of the United States in the decade before 9/11. It was bad advice then; it is worse advice now.

The critics are right about one thing: President Bush took an enormous risk in Iraq. The risk could well have gone wrong—and it could still go wrong. But wars are not won by leaders who think only about avoiding failure. Wars are won by leaders who dare to fight, as President Bush has dared and as his would-be successors evidently do not.

Nobody would claim that the United States made no mistakes in Iraq. When have we ever fought a war without mistakes?

Our defense planners expected that there would be a flood of hungry refugees from Iraq and prepared accordingly. Happily, they got that wrong. Our planners expected that Saddam's forces would surrender rather than run away. They got that wrong too, with rather worse effect, for the planners had hoped that those surrendered soldiers without human-rights offenses in their past could swiftly be formed into the nucleus of a new Iraqi police.

But of all our mistakes, probably the most serious was our unwillingness to allow the Iraqi National Congress, Iraq's leading anti-Saddam resistance movement, to form a provisional government after the fall of Baghdad. In 1944, we took care to let French troops enter Paris before U.S. or British forces. We should have shown equal tact in 2003. The INC offered us troops willing to fight and security forces ready to help keep order. We rebuffed the offer, in large part because the State Department and the CIA disliked Ahmed Chalabi, the INC's leader, and because the INC terrified the Saudis and therefore terrified those in our government who wished to placate the Saudis.

The State Department/CIA argument that Chalabi had no following in Iraq was wholly disingenuous. During Saddam's long reign of terror his opponents were exiled, murdered, or silent. Moreover, both State and the Agency had their preferred candidates—Adnan Pachachi in the case of State, Iyad Alawi in the case of the CIA—men who, like Chalabi, had lived outside

Iraq for many years. But Chalabi had spent long periods in northern Iraq, something the others had not done. And when he was abroad, rallying support for Saddam's overthrow, Chalabi lived with a price on his head, to which he was coolly, courageously indifferent. No, it was not the lack of support among Iraqis that led to bureaucratic disparagement of Ahmad Chalabi; the sad truth is that for the pettiest of reasons neither State nor the CIA liked Chalabi, despite his tireless and remarkably effective effort to organize and encourage opposition to Saddam's regime. In part they didn't like the fact that he was not a puppet they could easily control. In part they resented his many admirers among members of Congress of both parties. In part they disliked his low tolerance for bureaucrats who were largely ignorant of the situation in Iraq and the potential contribution that Saddam's opponents could make to Iraq's liberation. In part they were humiliated by the frequency with which Chalabi had been right and they had been wrong. One result of this disparagement was to limit the role of the Iraqi opposition in the liberation and postwar administration of Iraq, leaving the responsibility, and risks, disproportionately in the hands of Americans. Seldom has the foreign policy bureaucracy inflicted such shameful damage on American interests than in its opposition to working with Saddam's Iraqi opponents.

Without local allies, we were left to keep order in the cities and villages of Iraq with American soldiers. Our military is the best-equipped, best-trained fighting force in the history of the world. But our soldiers are not police: They do not speak the language, they do not know the customs, and they do not know which communal leaders can be trusted and which cannot.

Nobody who advocated the removal of Saddam Hussein imagined that Iraq would transform itself from brutal tyranny into a humane civil society overnight. It was anticipated that there would be lawlessness and worse. But what was *not* anticipated was that our State Department and CIA would extend their hostility to the Iraqi National Congress to the point where their bureaucratic dislikes deprived our forces in the field of crucial assistance.

Self-criticism is valuable, even essential. And yet we would be making an even more severe mistake of our own if we allowed necessary self-criticism to blind us to the steady flow of positive events in Iraq. A free press has been born. Schools have reopened, and the high school class of 2003 graduated on time. Electricity is being generated and distributed more reliably than at any time in Iraq's recent history. Oil is being produced and exported for the benefit of all Iraqis, not just a single dictator and his family. Town and village councils are being elected. A stable currency has been issued. A new judiciary is being recruited that will enforce and apply the rule of law. Soon Iraq will have a constitution and an elected leadership.

The struggle against extremism inside Iraq has not ended. Neither has the larger war on terror. We have come nowhere near the end of the war on terror, nowhere near the beginning of the end. At most, we have come (to borrow a phrase of Winston Churchill's) to the end of the beginning. Americans can take heart from what has been accomplished so far. They certainly deserve better than the disinformation and even calumny they hear from some critics of the Iraq war. But they will continue to need perseverance and courage for the struggles ahead—and those critics of the Iraq war who exhausted their stockpiles of perseverance and courage before the shooting even started have disqualified themselves from leadership in those struggles.

3. THE NEW AXIS

THERE IS NOTHING NEW about terrorism. What is new since 9/11 is the chilling realization that the terrorist threat we thought we had contained within tolerable boundaries was not contained at all, menacing our well-being as a people, even our survival as a nation.

This realization stems, first, from the scale of 9/11, and beyond that, from the apocalyptic vision of the terrorists themselves. The chill comes from knowing that there are, among the terrorists, hundreds and perhaps thousands who are ready to die in order to kill. They cannot be deterred. They cannot be appeased. The terrorists kill and will accept death for a cause with which no accommodation is possible.

That cause is militant Islam. Of the thirty-six organizations the U.S. Department of State designates as "foreign terrorist organizations," seventeen purport to act in the name of Islam, and six more are predominantly Muslim in membership.* Yet for many reasons our leaders, and the leaders of other nations,

---

* See the Appendix.

have found it difficult to say so. Like the wizards in *Harry Potter,* they dread pronouncing out loud the enemy's name. We sometimes wonder how the war on terror escaped being called "the war against You-know-who."

President Bush was right to insist that the United States has no quarrel with Islam. But while Americans have no proper quarrel with Islam, a radical strain within Islam has declared war on us. This strain seeks to overthrow our civilization and remake the nations of the West into Islamic societies, imposing on the whole world its religion and its law. To achieve these cosmic ambitions, Islamic terrorists wish—and are preparing—to commit murder on a horrific scale. On 9/11, al-Qaeda killed in a single day more people than the Irish Republican Army has killed in thirty-five years. Al-Qaeda and other Islamic terrorist groups feverishly seek chemical, biological, radiological, and nuclear weapons to kill on a yet larger scale. If they get them, they will use them.

And though it is comforting to deny it, all the available evidence indicates that militant Islam commands wide support, and even wider sympathy, among Muslims worldwide, including Muslim minorities in the West. A major opinion survey of nine Middle Eastern countries in early 2002 found that one-third of the population—even more in Kuwait and Saudi Arabia—refused to condemn the 9/11 attacks.*

In militant Islam, we face an aggressive ideology of world

---

* The poll was conducted by the Gallup Organization. Details are available at news.bbc.co.uk/1/hi/world/americas/1843838.stm.

domination. Like communism, this ideology perverts the language of justice and equality to justify oppression and murder. Like Nazism, it exploits the injured pride of once-mighty nations. Like both communism and Nazism, militant Islam is opportunistic—it works willingly with all manner of unlikely allies, as the communists and Nazis worked with each other against the democratic West.

Item: On June 2 and 3, 2002, the leaders of four major terrorist organizations, Hezbollah, Hamas, Islamic Jihad, and the Popular Front for the Liberation of Palestine general command (PFLPGC), convened in Teheran. Much analysis of the Middle East would suggest that this meeting could never have happened. Hezbollah, after all, is a Shiite extremist organization backed by Iran; Hamas is a Sunni terrorist group that draws its financial support from donors in Saudi Arabia and North America; Islamic Jihad is an even more fanatical Sunni group; and the PFLPGC is a Marxist-Leninist faction sponsored by the secular Baathists of Syria. Yet here they were, meeting in an Iranian conference center, discussing how to work together to annihilate Israel. Shortly afterward, President Clinton's former Middle East envoy, Dennis Ross, warned in a newspaper column that Iran was successfully pressuring Hamas, Islamic Jihad, and Hezbollah to coordinate their attacks on the Jewish state, confirming reports that Israeli intelligence had been issuing since 1999.*

* Dennis Ross, "The Hidden Threat in the Middle East," *The Wall Street Journal*, June 24, 2002, p. A14.

Item: When U.S. forces overthrew the Taliban in November 2001, Iran granted refuge to more than 250 senior al-Qaeda and Taliban figures, reportedly including Saad bin Laden, one of Osama's eldest sons, and Ayman al-Zawahiri, the Egyptian doctor who is widely believed to be the group's governing intelligence. (In June 2003, the Iranian government confirmed the presence of al-Qaeda figures in Iran but insisted that they had been "detained."* They are in fact operating in complete liberty.)

This too was something we were told could never happen. Iran and the Taliban were supposedly deadly enemies. In 1998, Iran and Afghanistan had nearly gone to war over the murder of nine Iranian diplomats and the Taliban's maltreatment of Afghan Shiites. The Bureau of Near East Affairs at the Department of State even promised that we could expect help from Iran in countering the Taliban regime. As for al-Qaeda, it is connected to the terrorist groups in Pakistan that intersperse their attacks on Kashmir with anti-Shiite atrocities like the July 2003 massacre of forty-seven worshippers at a mosque in Quetta. Yet as soon as the United States attacked the Taliban and al-Qaeda, the Iranians rushed to support them.

Item: The Baathists of Syria and Iraq have been rivals since the late 1960s. Syria even joined the anti-Iraq coalition in 1991. Yet Syria sold supplies to Saddam's armies to prepare for the 2003 war, gave shelter to Saddam's officials and members of his family after the war, and has allowed its territory to be

---

* www.time.com/time/world/article/0,8599,198857,00.html.

traversed by pro-Saddam guerrillas recruited by several terrorist organizations on their way to fight U.S. forces rebuilding Iraq. Syria is a secular dictatorship—but it hosts Hezbollah in Lebanon and permits it to maintain offices in Damascus.

Item: North Korea is one of the world's last remaining Marxist-Leninist states, militantly atheistic. Iran is an Islamic theocracy. Yet these two supposedly antipathetic regimes are sharing nuclear and missile technology. As recently as March, April, and May 2003, representatives of the Iranian government visited North Korea to seek assistance for their nuclear program.* In December 2002, Spanish warships on patrol in the Indian Ocean stopped a freighter carrying North Korean missiles to Yemen under a falsified cargo manifest. At the inexplicable urging of the State Department, the missiles were released for delivery.

It is now often claimed that President Bush has repudiated any connection between al-Qaeda and Saddam Hussein. This is simply false. President Bush did tell reporters on September 17, 2003, that there was "no evidence" that Saddam was involved with the 9/11 attacks. If "evidence" means "proof," then the president was right: The clues and hints we have linking Saddam's intelligence to the hijackers are inconclusive. But they are not nonexistent.

They include the fact that Czech intelligence remains convinced that Mohammed Atta met Iraqi intelligence officer Ahmad Khalil Ibrahim Samir al-Ani in Prague in April 2001.

* Philip Webster, "Britain Takes Steps to Curb Iran's Nuclear Ambitions," *The Times,* June 13, 2003, p. 1.

Saddam's foreign minister, Tariq Aziz, offered an extraordinary nondenial denial of the Atta–al-Ani meeting: "Even if such an incident had taken place, it doesn't mean anything. Any diplomat in any mission might meet people in a restaurant here or there and talk to them, which is meaningless. If that person turned out to be something else, that doesn't mean he had a connection with what that person did later."

And we know that Iraq's Czech embassy *was* involved in terrorism: Al-Ani's predecessor (one Jabir Salim) defected to the West in December 1998 and revealed a plot to blow up the Radio Free Europe transmitter in Prague.

Even if we agree to catalog the Atta/Iraq story as an unsolved mystery, pending further investigations in the Iraqi archives, it remains true—*as President Bush also said on September 17*—that there is "no question that Saddam had al-Qaeda ties."

In 1998, bin Laden and the Iraqi government opened discussions on a joint campaign against the United States, according to documents found in Iraq by the British newspaper the *Daily Telegraph* in April 2003.* More recently, intelligence sources have received credible information that Ayman al-Zawahiri visited Baghdad in 1998 and received a $300,000 payment just before he merged his Egyptian Islamic Jihad group with bin Laden's al-Qaeda.[†]

* Inigo Gilmore, "The Proof That Saddam Worked with bin Laden: Documents Found in Iraqi Intelligence HQ Detail Meetings with al-Qaeda Envoys," *Sunday Telegraph,* April 27, 2003, p. 1.

[†] See Stephen Hayes, "Saddam's al Qaeda Connection," *The Weekly Standard,* September 8, 2003, available at www.theweeklystandard.com/Content/Public/Articles/000/000/003/033jgqyi.asp.

Unearthing the links between bin Laden and Saddam Hussein would have been hard work under any circumstances. But the persistent opposition of the CIA and the DIA to any outside investigation of those links made the task all the more difficult. When a small team of independent analysts inside the Office of the Secretary of Defense found clues that had eluded the agencies, the CIA and DIA sprang into action. First, they tried to deny the independent analysts essential access to the information they needed to do their work. Then they ferociously cross-examined every link the independent analysts did find—as if they were more concerned to defend their vested opinion than to hear new observations. Next, they waged a campaign of leaks that accused the independent analysts—all four of them—of forming a "cabal" and "politicizing" intelligence. Finally, they cooked up specious charges and removed the security clearance of at least one of the analysts.

But, if anyone bent intelligence, it was those analysts at the CIA and DIA who allowed their assumptions about what Saddam Hussein and Osama bin Laden would do and would not do to blind them to important information. And when challenged, they reacted with unprofessional vindictiveness.

Nobody denies the reality of the religious, ideological, and ethnic divisions of the Middle East. But the willingness of terrorist groups and terror states to cooperate with one another despite these divisions is also a reality. And why should that be surprising? Each faction has its own utopia to offer— but each is appealing to the same grievances and competing for the same constituency. The radicals may detest one another, but their murderous hatred of the United States pushes all lesser animosities aside.

Where does this hatred come from? In the first shock after the terrorist attack, many journalists took it on themselves to repeat the long list of Middle Eastern and Islamic grievances against the United States—and repeated them in a way that implied that these grievances were understandable, even legitimate.

The United States surely has made mistakes in the Middle East, as it has elsewhere in the world. But a hatred as all-consuming and self-destructive as the hatred encountered in radical Islam tells us much more about those who hate than about the one who is hated. Middle Eastern terrorism may have seized on the United States as its target, but the roots of Muslim rage are to be found in Islam itself.

Unlike Christianity, Islam offers its believers rewards on earth as well as in heaven. Adherents of the true faith are assured of victory on the battlefield and economic and cultural supremacy in the world: "Allah has promised to those of you who believe and do good that He will most certainly make them rulers in the earth as He made rulers those before them. . . ."* For more than two centuries, these triumphant promises have proven false. The Islamic world has lagged further and further behind the Christian West; since 1948, it has repeatedly been humiliated even by the once disdained Jews. These defeats and disasters have been more than a wound to

* The Koran, sura 24, "The Light," verse 55.

Muslims: They directly challenge the truth of Islam itself. And no nation poses a more comprehensive challenge to the vision and ambition of radical Islam than the United States, a secular, democratic, Judeo-Christian, sexually egalitarian superpower.

The United States first arrived in the Middle East as a major power during World War II. It was not a propitious introduction. We were allies of the British and Free French; local opinion had strongly backed the Germans. The Nazis had promised to liberate the Arab world from Anglo-French colonial rule, and Nazi views on the Jewish question were widely approved in the region. In 1941, a pro-Nazi regime seized power in Baghdad and had to be ejected by a British military intervention—but only after the regime incited an anti-Jewish pogrom that killed two hundred people and terrorized and impoverished one of the oldest Jewish communities in the Arab world. The defeat of the Baghdad coup deterred overt pro-German militancy for the remainder of the war, but there could be no doubt which side had won the battle for Arab hearts and minds. The religious leader of the Palestinian Arabs, the grand mufti of Jerusalem, Haj-Amin al-Husseini, took refuge in Germany in 1941, met Hitler, and made propaganda broadcasts on the Germans' behalf. In 1947, two nationalistic young Syrians, one Christian and one Muslim, founded the Baath ("Renaissance") Party in Damascus, to promote an Arab awakening based on fascist ideals and ideology. Throughout the Arab world, idealistic young officers—including the future peacemaker Anwar Sadat—

plotted how they might sabotage the British and French and help the German armies.

After the war, the United States pressed Britain and France to grant independence to their Arab colonies. In the Suez crisis of 1956, President Eisenhower broke with our French and British allies to side with Egypt. President John F. Kennedy, in his turn, forcefully supported the Algerian insurrection against France. But American anticolonialism did the United States little good with Arab opinion. Americans might repudiate the heavy-handed methods of the British and the French, but American power only too obviously supported the political order the British and French had created. Hardly any of the countries on the map of the postwar Middle East existed before 1920; hardly any of them had ever existed at all. The territory we call Iraq had not constituted an integral political unit since the days of the Assyrians. Syria was the name of a Roman province. Algeria, Jordan, Kuwait, and Libya were the fancies of imperialist cartographers. Only Egypt, Iran, Morocco, and Turkey could claim frontiers that made any geographic or historical sense. But even these four relatively stable states were the stumps of vanished empires, sometimes applying brutal force to the unrecognized ethnic and linguistic minorities trapped within their artificial borders. As for Saudi Arabia, what was it but a gigantic real estate claim on behalf of one lucky family, like the King Ranch, only bigger and with oil? Yet in the name of stability, anticommunism, and secure fuel supplies, the United States stood ready to guard those boundaries against all challengers. And within these boundaries, the United States found itself (usually reluctantly and often unavailingly) lending its support to the selfsame elites that had been installed originally by the British or the French.

In other words, from the point of view of the people of the Middle East, the United States looked like the colonialists' successor. Partly for that reason, many Arabs continued to blame the United States for its role in the creation of the state of Israel long after they had forgiven the Soviet Union for its even larger contribution. The Soviet Union recognized the independence of Israel in 1948 two days after the United States and denounced the ensuing Arab invasion more vehemently than the U.S. government. The weapons with which the Israelis won their war of independence were provided mostly by the Soviet bloc. Not until 1962 did the United States make its first major arms sale to Israel, and not until 1970 did the United States extend aid for the purchase of military equipment. Indeed, until 1967, France was Israel's major arms supplier and Germany its single largest source of economic aid. (By then, of course, the Soviets had long since switched sides.)

But if Americans were the colonialists' successors, we were obviously colonialists of a new type. Compared to the British, the French, and our Soviet cold war enemy, we respected the individual sovereignties of the countries of the Middle East. When asked to leave, we left, as we left Libya in 1970 after the new government of Colonel Muammar al-Qaddafi ordered us to evacuate Wheelus Field. This record of deference helped to persuade Anwar Sadat to expel his overbearing Soviet advisers in 1971 and reorient Egypt toward the United States.

Again, unlike the British and French, the United States hesitated to deploy military power in the region. When our Arab friends got into trouble, we delegated the job of protecting them—to Britain (which airlifted troops to Kuwait when Iraq threatened the newly independent emirate in 1961), to Israel (which mobilized to deter the Syrians from attacking Jordan's King Hussein in 1970), and to Iran (which policed the Gulf for the United States in the 1970s). In the forty-five years from the end of World War II to the end of the cold war, significant numbers of American troops were sent into the Middle East only twice, in 1958 and 1983, and both times to the one country in the region with a large Christian population and a history of welcoming Western influence, Lebanon.* This light touch did not necessarily win us friends in the Middle East, but it did at least present a smaller target for the region's xenophobes and fanatics.

With Nazi Germany out of contention, those xenophobes and fanatics turned to the Soviet Union for inspiration. In Iraq, the Communist Party emerged as the nation's strongest political organization. The communists mobilized a million marchers on May Day 1959 and for a moment looked poised to seize power. In the 1960s, the governments of Egypt, Syria, and Algeria declared themselves "socialist republics." Left-

---

* A small detachment of peacekeepers was also sent to the Sinai in 1982, with the agreement of both Israel and Egypt, to monitor the U.S.-brokered disengagement between them.

wing ideology swept through the region's universities like smallpox ravaging a virgin population.

Revolutionary Marxism offered hope that Arabs could obtain the benefits of modernity without the humiliation of Westernization, as it was then believed the Soviets had done. Revolutionary Marxism conjured up a seductive vision of progress without compromise with the wealthy West.

And for one spectacular moment, the dream that Arab militancy might enable the Middle East to seize for itself the wealth and power of the West did appear plausible. The Arab oil embargo of 1973, the oil price explosion of 1974, and the emergence of the Organization of Petroleum Exporting Countries (OPEC) dealt the industrialized world a blow that sent it staggering. For the first time in eight hundred years, the Arabs had succeeded in inflicting pain on the West, rather than the other way around. Money flooded into the oil-producing states, although oil revenues were hardly shared equitably. Still, the governments of the Persian Gulf constructed roads and universities and created well-paid, undemanding civil service jobs for their citizens, while dispensing carefully controlled sums to poorer Arab governments and organizations. Western corporations and governments paid humble tribute to the new lords of oil, and sycophantic Western authors wrote books hailing the supremacy of the petro-powers. Arab demands and complaints sprang to the top of the world agenda—and Arab crimes and atrocities dropped to the bottom. Between January 1972 and January 1974, European police forces apprehended fifty suspected Arab terrorists. Of those fifty, only seven saw the inside of a prison. Thirty-six were released without trial, including the surviving members of the Palestinian terror squad that murdered the Israeli Olympic team at Munich in 1972.

But the hopes of the 1970s soon proved illusory. The petropowers had not gained power, only wealth, and unearned wealth at that. The oil paid for a lavish flow of imported goods and for the menial labor of contract workers from South Asia and the Philippines; for extravagant apartments in London, Paris, the Côte d'Azur, and New York; and for the latest weapons systems—but it did not create dynamic economies, a sense of nationhood, or the military skill to use the weapons. Nor could oil bring victory over Israel. In two days of fighting over Lebanon in 1982, the Israeli air force shot down ninety-six Syrian warplanes without losing a single one of its own. Egypt signed a separate peace in 1979. Oil did not even bring with it the know-how to keep the oil flowing. The Arab oil producers remained as abjectly dependent as ever on Western expertise. The new petropowers painfully discovered that they had become petrotargets: targets for aggrieved and radicalized fellow Arabs like the Palestinians; targets for external predators like the Soviet Union; targets for their own people, whose expectations would have been hard enough to satisfy even if the price of oil had kept rising, rather than collapsing as it did in 1986. Between 1980 and 2000, Saudi Arabia's gross domestic product (GDP) per person, adjusted for inflation, shrank by almost half. To put it another way: In 1980, the average Saudi income equaled the average Israeli income; by 2000, the average Saudi income had tumbled to about *one-third* that of the average Israeli.* In oil- and gas-rich Algeria, the unemployment rate hit 34 percent in 2002.

In the boom days of the 1970s, rising incomes had disrupted traditional authority and incited envy, resentment, and rebellion. Now, as the economies of the Arab world imploded, their societies plunged into an abyss of cruelty and terror. The Islamic revolution of 1979 had brought a ferocious new regime to power in Iran; that same year, Saddam Hussein grabbed sole power in Iraq. Iraq invaded Iran in 1980; the war lasted eight years and killed or maimed more than a million people. Even before his battles against Iran ended, Saddam launched a campaign of massacre in the Kurdish area of northern Iraq, gassing to death as many as five thousand people in the town of Halabja and killing perhaps one hundred thousand Kurds altogether. In 1992, Algeria convulsed into a civil war that destroyed hundreds of villages and left at least forty thousand of its people dead. Even where outright civil or foreign war was avoided, dictators and would-be dictators piled up the corpses in their struggles to gain and hold power. In 1982, the Assad dictatorship brutally crushed Islamic rebellions in the Syrian cities of Hamah and Aleppo. In three weeks of fighting, certainly ten thousand and

---

* All figures are from the World Bank, in constant 1995 dollars. Saudi GDP per capita 1980: $11,557. Israeli GDP per capita 1980: $11,592. Saudi GDP per capita 2000: $6,728. Israeli GDP per capita 2000: $17,067. The World Bank statistics are conservative: Some Western analysts contend that Saudi GNP per person may have dropped by as much as 70 percent over the 1980–2000 period.

maybe as many as twenty thousand civilians were wiped out by the army's shells and bullets.

The Middle East is not the only region of the world buffeted by violence and chaos. But unlike in Africa or Central America, oil wealth makes the Middle East strategically essential. And unlike the leaders of countries in Africa or Central America, Middle Eastern rulers can afford to try to buy protection from their neighbors—and their own people—by investing in ever deadlier technologies of war, including, ultimately, weapons of mass destruction.

As the region spiraled into self-inflicted chaos and ever bloodier conflicts, and as its worst regimes raced faster and faster to acquire nuclear weapons, the old American practice of maintaining a low profile became more and more difficult to sustain. Like a would-be rescuer in the grip of a drowning man, the United States was pulled deeper and deeper into the region's vortex of paranoia and hatred.

When Iraq invaded Iran in 1980, Henry Kissinger quipped, "It's a pity they both can't lose." But then Iran tried to pressure Iraq's Arab allies by firing missiles at tankers and the U.S. Navy had to be called in to protect the flow of oil. Kuwaiti vessels were allowed to fly the U.S. flag, and an American flotilla steamed into the Gulf to ensure that vessels flying the flag went unmolested. American ships traded fire with Iranian boats and aircraft. In July 1988, a U.S. cruiser, the *Vincennes,* accidentally shot down an Iranian civilian airliner. The United States apologized and paid compensation, but the Iranians misinterpreted the awful tragedy as a signal that the United States was preparing to intervene directly against them—one motive for their decision to make peace with Iraq the next month.

In 1990, Iraq invaded Kuwait, and for the first time in half a century, American soldiers came to the Middle East to fight. The Americans had landed—and they stayed. The American troops arrived in the Middle East at the same time as satellite television and the Internet, and just as hundreds of thousands of young Muslims were abandoning their countries to migrate to the wealthy West.

By a poignant coincidence, the decade in which the Arab and Muslim Middle East tumbled into economic stagnation and mass mutual slaughter was the same decade in which the United States hurtled into one of its periodic technological sprints. At the launch of Operation Desert Storm, American computers still ran DOS, mobile phones were expensive luxuries, and fashionable intellectuals were predicting the collapse of American power. "The cold war is over—Germany and Japan won," quipped Paul Tsongas, winner of the New Hampshire Democratic primary in 1992. Six years later, when Osama bin Laden announced his anti-American fatwa, American primacy looked more unassailable than at any time since the Eisenhower administration. One final twist of the knife: Just as America was ascending these heights of supremacy, the Marxist ideology that had inspired the Middle East's dissident intellectuals collapsed. Even the wildest anti-American in the coffeehouses of Cairo and Beirut had to admit that there was no alternative, non-Western route to the future. If an alternative was to be found, it was to be found in the past, in a return to Islam—not Islam as it ever actually was, but a new, politicized Islam: Islam as an ideology.

Some scholars call ideological Islam "Islamism," to emphasize the sharp contrast between this new militant creed and the Islam of the past. Islamic extremists may quote ancient scripture, or speak archaic Arabic, or dress as they imagine Muhammad's warriors might have dressed thirteen hundred years ago. But they remain men of the twentieth and twenty-first centuries, imbued despite themselves with the ideas and doctrines of their own time. And the most influential of those twentieth-century ideas has been the liberating power of violence and destruction. "Violence is a cleansing force," Frantz Fanon announced in his hugely influential 1961 manifesto in praise of third world revolution, *The Wretched of the Earth*. Only violence "frees the native from his inferiority complex and from his despair and inactivity: It makes him fearless and restores his self-respect."* Shortly after the 9/11 attacks, bin Laden released a videotape exulting over the destruction of the Twin Towers. "The values of this Western civilization under the leadership of America have been destroyed. Those awesome symbolic terrors that speak of liberty, human rights, and humanity have been destroyed. They have gone up in smoke." Restoring injured pride through the destruction of the symbols of an opposing civilization: Bin Laden did it, but he was by no means the first to wish for it.

---

* *The Wretched of the Earth* (Grove, 1961), p. 94.

Generations of extremist leaders in the Middle East—fascists, communists, pan-Arabists, now Islamists—have each in their turn made a bid to lead a unified East against the enemy West. Bin Laden follows where the grand mufti of Jerusalem, Gamal Abdel Nasser, Muammar al-Qaddafi, the Ayatollah Ruhollah Khomeini, and Saddam Hussein have preceded him. Bin Laden offers a new answer, but it is an answer to the same question.

Three decades of Saudi-funded Islamic education have prepared the minds of millions of young Middle Easterners to accept bin Laden's answer and celebrate killing on a vaster scale than anything ever contemplated in the region before. Unnumbered billions of dollars have flowed from the Saudi government and from Saudi religious foundations to radical Islamic academies throughout the Middle East and around the world. A Tunisian intellectual, Afif Al-Akhdar, has warned that "the Saudi curriculum brainwashes the pupil of any suspect rationality that might infect him . . . [and] sows among the children the seeds of the culture of hatred for the Jews and the Christians." Wherever the Saudi infrastructure of incitement reaches, from Indonesia to Indiana, it inculcates "contempt for the rational, for women, and for non-Muslims; yearning for the Caliphate state; liberating Palestine to the last grain of earth; and regaining Andalusia and establishing an Islamic regime in France within the next 50 years!"*

Religious extremists and secular militants; Sunnis and

* www.memri.org/bin/latestnews.cgi?ID=SD57603.

Shiites; communists and fascists—in the Middle East, these categories blend into one another. All gush from the same enormous reservoir of combustible rage. And all have the same target: the United States.

This murderous rage must be met and defeated on three fronts: at home, where it attempts to penetrate our defenses and murder our people; abroad, where it inspires governments and terrorist groups to plot nuclear and biological jihad against us; and, finally, in the minds of the men and women if the Islamic world.

4. THE WAR AT HOME

THE WAR ON terror cannot be won at home, but it can be lost here. It is here that the terrorists hope to inflict a devastating blow that will kill thousands, topple the U.S. economy, and destroy Americans' will to fight; here that they hope to win a victory that will embolden the angry millions of the Muslim world to join their jihad. Merely averting the blow is no substitute for victory. But failing to avert the blow will push us a long way to defeat.

Tally the number and variety of potential targets in the United States, and the task of defending the country seems beyond human capacity. How to protect dozens of nuclear power plants and hundreds of petroleum refineries, chemical factories of every kind, and tens of thousands of miles of natural gas pipeline? There are trains to derail and buses to hijack, tunnels to poison and bridges to detonate, and thousands of commercial and private air flights per day. There are as many ways to spread biological poisons as there are places where people eat, drink, or breathe: A sufficiently suicidal terrorist could infect *himself* with smallpox and then spend a day riding the New York subway, potentially communicating the disease to everyone in every car he entered. Coordinated cyberterror attacks could jam 911 systems with false alerts and paralyze public health systems at the time of a real attack. And so on and on it goes, through all the possibilities that might occur to the minds of fanatics and mass murderers.

Yet the United States may be a tougher target than it looks. If we were to ask the Department of Homeland Security to issue a comprehensive edict to protect every vulnerable point in the country, the task would be about as hopeless as an old Soviet central plan. But that's not how Americans do things. The nation entrusts the first responsibility for the safety of each nuclear power plant, each chemical factory, each petroleum refinery, and each natural gas pipeline to those who know that plant, that factory, that refinery, and that pipeline best: its owners and employees. If the terrorists want to try to blow up a nuclear power plant, they must match their wits against people who have devoted their lives to the problem of nuclear safety. Ditto for chemicals, ditto for refineries, ditto for pipelines. In the movies, terrorists are skilled specialists; in real life, most of them are amateurs who do boneheaded things like return to collect the security deposit on the rental truck they have just exploded—which is how the World Trade Center conspirators of 1993 were caught. The terrorists' most important advantage was our complacency, and after 9/11 that advantage was lost for good. The American push to adapt and to innovate, the remorseless drive for improvement, is now mobilized as a mighty weapon of defense against terrorists.

Unfortunately, many Democrats in Congress seem to be interested less in defending the homeland than in preparing to recover after the next terrorist disaster. In a March 2003 statement, Senator Patrick Leahy of Vermont called for a huge increase in spending on local police, fire, and emergency departments, to be funded, if we read the senator correctly, by reducing spending on antiterrorist operations abroad: "When terrorists strike, first responders are and will always be the first people we turn to. . . . We read almost daily about the Administration's apparent eagerness to provide untold billions of additional dollars for foreign governments in the war on terrorism. But our first responders are told to make do with a small fraction of those sums."* Of course, the country should be well prepared to care for those injured by terrorist attack, and Congress should make available whatever funds are necessary to the task. (Though Congress should also be appropriately alert to the tendency of many cash-strapped state and local governments to repackage almost everything they do as "first response" in order to qualify for more federal aid.) But important as it is to be prepared to help the wounded and injured after a terrorist attack, it is far more important to prevent the terrorist attack in the first place. As George Patton could have said, "Nobody ever won a war by caring for his wounded. He won by making the other poor SOB care for *his* wounded."

To stop terrorists before they strike, we must do three

---

* leahy.senate.gov/press/200303/030403a.html.

things: deny them entry into the country, curtail their freedom of action inside the country, and deprive them of material and moral support from within the country.

Denying Terrorists Entry into the United States

ISLAMIC TERRORISM IS a foreign threat that has domesticated itself within our borders. To strike targets on American soil, the terrorists must cross an American border. Unfortunately, those borders have been wide open, and even now are laxly guarded.

For example: The leader of the 9/11 hijackers, Mohammed Atta, was caught in January 2001 at Miami International Airport attempting to enter the United States illegally. Atta's tourist visa had expired, and his application for a student visa had not yet been approved. There were other irregularities in his status as well—yet the officer on duty waved him through.

Another example: Omar Abdel Rahman, the blind sheikh who instigated the 1993 World Trade Center bombing and plots to blow up New York landmarks, was actually on a CIA terrorist watch list when he applied for a tourist visa in the 1980s. He then falsified his name, applied for a permanent resident visa as a "minister of religion"—and got it.

A third example: Of the forty-eight foreign-born extremists who have been convicted or who have confessed to involvement in Islamic terrorist plots since 1993 (including the nineteen 9/11 hijackers), twelve were present in the United

States illegally at the time of their attack, and nearly half had violated the immigration laws in some important way at some point before their attack.* In other words, vigorous enforcement of the *existing immigration laws* would probably have foiled not only 9/11 but almost all the earlier terrorist attacks as well.

Since 9/11, the United States has taken some faltering steps to enhance the enforcement of those laws.

The CIA is doing more to keep the terrorist watch list updated. (Khalid al-Midhar, one of the 9/11 hijackers, entered the United States early in 2000 and left later that year. In January 2001, the CIA learned of his involvement in the attack on the USS *Cole*. Yet it did not get around to placing him on the watch list until August 2001. Had the CIA acted faster, al-Midhar could have been halted at the border when he returned in July 2001.)

Visa requirements are being enforced more strictly. Visa applications from twenty-five predominantly Muslim countries, including Saudi Arabia, are now for the first time being systematically checked against the FBI's terrorist database. The Immigration and Naturalization Service has pledged to have up and working by 2005 a computer system that can track whether visa holders actually leave the country at the time they are obliged to go. And federal authorities are for the first time making a serious effort to locate the three hun-

---

* Steven A. Camarota, "The Open Door: How Militant Islamic Terrorists Entered and Remained in the United States, 1993–2001," Center for Immigration Studies Paper #21. We have relied on the CIS's excellent work throughout this section.

dred thousand or so immigrants who remain in this country even after they were ordered deported.

This is progress—often achieved reluctantly, but still progress. Nevertheless, infiltrating potential terrorists into the United States remains troublingly easy and, as things now stand, is likely to remain so.

This is not the first time, for example, that the INS has attempted to keep track of whether temporary visa holders leave when scheduled. It tried repeatedly in the 1990s, foundering again and again on the opposition of the Clinton administration, its own choking and inept bureaucracy, and—maybe most important—the hostility of the universities. Suppose a student has been granted a visa for an academic year, September to June. If he fails to exit the country as scheduled in June, the new INS computers may or may not register the fact. But suppose he drops out of class in October and disappears? Who but the university will be aware that he has violated the terms of his visa? Yet many of our universities refuse on principle to cooperate in any way with the immigration authorities. As for other categories of temporary visa, such as the business visas favored by the 9/11 hijackers, there is no U.S. institution that has even as much ability to monitor them as the universities have with student visas. Anyway, a visa system is only as good as the database against which it is checked. At the time that Zacarias Moussaoui applied for a student visa to study at a U.S. flight school, the French government knew of his extremist background, but it did not share the knowledge with the United States.

Nor would it be wise to place too much trust in even the best visa system as a means of defense. France, Germany, Britain, and Canada all host significant numbers of Islamic extremists. Yet there is no visa requirement for travelers from Europe and Canada, and it would be intolerably burdensome to U.S. commerce and tourism to impose one. Even if the United States did do such a destructive thing, terrorists could still elude it—as hundreds of thousands of illegal immigrants do every year—by slipping across the border by foot, by truck, or by container ship. Alternatively, the terrorists could defeat the requirement, because the visa system checks only for undesired *names,* not for unchangeable features like fingerprints.

Having defeated the visa system, terrorists can then join the perhaps eight million or so illegal immigrants whose presence inside the country is tacitly permitted by federal, state, and local authorities. They can open bank accounts, obtain driver's licenses, take jobs, and effectively vanish from view. If they are caught breaking the law, the arresting officers will probably not inquire into their immigration status—in fact, in September 2003 New York City mayor Michael Bloomberg issued an executive order that forbade New York police or any other agency of the city government ever to cooperate with federal immigration law, except in cases of violent crime or in the investigation of known terrorists. Los Angeles and other cities have similar policies. And if the would-be terrorist applies for a job, as earlier and less well-funded terrorists have done, he will probably not be asked many questions then, either, for the law imposes few sanctions on employers who hire illegals.

Americans take a self-contradictory attitude toward immigration. They want the federal government to guard the borders. Let the illegal migrant cross the border, however, and the immigration laws cease to be enforced at all. Immigration is like a children's game in which the players are home free once they step over the magic line.

We ought to learn a lesson from the most effective anti-crime program the United States has ever seen: Mayor Rudolph Giuliani's crackdown in New York. Giuliani's core insight was this: People who break one law will break other laws. You want to catch a guy who's skipped out on a manslaughter arrest warrant? Stop every turnstile jumper and inspect his ID. You want to find the killer who left his fingerprints on a knife that stabbed a kid to death yesterday? Scan the fingerprints of everybody you catch smoking marijuana in the park today. In the same way: You want to find people who have entered the United States illegally with intent to commit massive crimes? Integrate immigration enforcement with *all* law enforcement, federal, state, and local, so that police can quickly and reliably check the immigration status of everyone they have grounds to stop and question.

Three of the 9/11 hijackers, for example, had brushes with the law in the months leading up to the terrorist attack. Hani Hanjour was stopped for speeding in Arlington, Virginia, on August 1, 2001. He presented police with a Florida driver's license. Police checked the license and found no warrants outstanding for him, so they let him go. What their search did not reveal was that Hanjour was living in the United States illegally. He had come into the country in 1996 and stayed for four years without papers, then reentered in 2000 on a student visa and never attended class. Had Hanjour been arrested and questioned, it might have disrupted the entire plot. Instead, he probably piloted American Airlines flight 77 into the Pentagon.

Mohammed Atta also carried a Florida driver's license. He was stopped for speeding in July 2001. He too lacked a valid visa at the time. The traffic stop failed to turn up this derogatory information (it did not even reveal that he had skipped out on a previous ticket and that a neighboring county had issued a warrant for his arrest!), and he too was released.

Finally, just two days before 9/11, police in Arlington, Virginia, stopped Ziad Jarrah for driving ninety in a sixty-five-miles-per-hour zone. Jarrah's status in the country was regular at the time—he had a valid tourist visa—but had police known that status, they might still have wondered how and why a Lebanese tourist had obtained a Virginia driver's license. If you visited Lebanon, would you apply for a Lebanese license? They might even have detained him long enough to discover that he had given the Virginia licensing authorities a false address. And that might have led to more questions—and maybe the unraveling of the plot.

We need an identification system that makes it clear who is entitled to be in the United States and who is not and that expedites the removal of people who are not so entitled. And there is only one system that will do the job: a national identity card that registers the bearer's name and biometric data, like fingerprints or retinal scans or DNA, and that indicates whether the bearer is a citizen, a permanent resident, or a temporary resident—and, if temporary, would indicate whether the bearer is permitted to work and the date by which he or she is supposed to leave. Resident aliens already carry a primitive version of such a card; it is time now to extend it to all lawful permanent and temporary residents of the United States.

We well understand and sympathize with the libertarian distaste for such a card. Though it is always possible that a national identity system could be used in abusive ways, one must measure the risk of abuse, and the harm that would come from it, and the difficulty of remedying that harm, against the continuing danger that is inherent in our inability accurately to identify potential terrorists. The victims of executive branch abuse will be able to sue the wrongdoers and collect damages; the victims of a mass terrorist attack will have no such recourse.

Anyway, the United States already has a system of national identification; it just happens to be a system that is easily manipulated: the local driver's license. A driver's license will be accepted at face value just about anywhere that identification is required, even at the gates of the White House. With it, you can, as Zacarias Moussaoui did, open a bank account and receive thousands of dollars in wire transfers from abroad. You can, as those three 9/11 hijackers discovered, emerge from a traffic stop no further questions asked. And you can, of course, use it to board a plane. Yet in the District of Columbia, the only proof of identity one needs to obtain a license is a lease and a utility bill. In Virginia, you do not need even that, just a buddy who will vouch that you are who you say you are and live where you claim to live. (This trusting attitude toward the most useful document an American carries explains why so many of the 9/11 hijackers obtained their licenses in the Old Dominion.) California tried to go further still: In September 2003, embattled governor Gray Davis signed a law intended to help illegal aliens obtain driver's licenses. Davis's law allowed foreign driver's licenses to be used as identification—practically an engraved invitation to foreign intelligence services to make themselves at home in the nation's largest state.

Americans are fighting to defend their liberty. None of us wants to live in a country where the authorities snoop on the people. But on those occasions when individuals can lawfully be asked to identify themselves—when they are stopped for a moving violation or some other infraction—the identification should establish that we genuinely are who we claim to be. Law-abiding citizens value privacy. Terrorists require invisibility. The two are not the same, and they should not be confused.

Information such as that which might have intercepted Khalid al-Midhar would become far more useful if an alien's identity could be checked reliably against the terrorist watch list every time he or she encountered the authorities: at a traffic stop, when boarding a flight inside the United States, or when applying for an extension of a tourist visa. Under such a system, we could worry a lot less about visitors from countries from which we do not require visas. Right now, a British citizen can fly to Orlando, no visa required; tell the immigration official that he plans to visit Disney World; rent an apartment under an assumed name; obtain a driver's license; and disappear. But under a system of national identity cards, he would not be able to disappear for long.

As Americans intensify their vigilance inside the borders, they also need to expand the definition of those activities that cause them to be suspicious at the border. Right now, American law bars the admission of aliens suspected of terrorist *activity*—but not of terrorist *sympathies*. In general, it is forbidden to deny admission to a would-be visitor to the United States for expressing political or religious views that would be protected under the First Amendment if he or she were an American citizen. An American citizen can preach sermons calling for the destruction of the United States, or praise Osama bin Laden at a public rally, or keep company with persons accused of terrorist acts, or collect a scientific library about toxins and poisons, or all four. American law indulgently allows a would-be visitor to the United States to do the same. While it remains theoretically possible to deny a visa to a prospective visitor with extremist views, the decision to exclude must be made by the secretary of state personally and must then be reported to Congress. Paperwork deters: As a practical matter, terrorist sympathizers are almost never excluded.

It should be obvious that the people most likely to engage in Islamic terrorism are those who believe what Islamic terrorists believe. Yet so anxious are we to avoid repeating the errors of the McCarthy period, when Congress passed an overzealous law that banned all members of foreign Communist parties from U.S. soil, that we now hesitate to take protective measures against even the most egregiously menacing people. It's a sobering thought that Ayman al-Zawahiri—who not only was al-Qaeda's number two man but had actually spent time in an Egyptian prison on suspicion of involvement in the assassination of Anwar Sadat—was able to enter the United States in 1995 for a cross-country fund-raising tour.

Curtailing Terrorists' Freedom of Action

THE PATRIOT ACT grants the FBI the ability to conduct twenty-first-century surveillance of terrorist suspects. It is temporary legislation—many of its provisions expire in 2005—so that Congress can return to the matter later, investigate whether abuses have taken place, and then revise the law accordingly. There's much to be said for this kind of "sunset" law. It took Congress until the mid-1970s to get around to formally terminating the state of belligerency it declared in April 1917, and World War I ended much more dramatically than the war on terrorism is likely to do.

But it was not a general wariness of obsolescence that caused the Patriot Act to be made temporary, but a very specific fear that the passions of the moment might stampede us into doing something "hysterical." Two years on, however, it is those fears of hysteria that themselves look hysterical. Civil liberties in the United States continue robust. The privacy of the American home is many millions of times more likely to be invaded by an e-mail spammer or a telemarketer than a federal agent. The right to dissent flourishes unrestrained—indeed, to judge by the way some of President Bush's wilder opponents carry on, it flourishes unrestrained even by common politeness or basic accuracy.

All of this is as it should be. Yet in our appropriate zeal to preserve and defend the right to speak freely and think differently, there is a real danger that Americans will make the opposite mistake. We may be so eager to protect the right to dissent that we lose sight of the difference between dissent and subversion; so determined to defend the right of privacy that we refuse to acknowledge even the most blatant warnings of danger.

Daniel Pipes of the Middle East Forum in Philadelphia is one of this country's most knowledgeable and rigorous experts on Islamic extremism. He recently reported the following story. In March 2003, federal agents, guns drawn, arrested an electrical engineer named Maher Mofeid "Mike" Hawash in the parking lot of the Oregon building in which he worked. Hawash, a Palestinian who had immigrated to the United States from Kuwait in 1984, was a valued employee of Intel. He earned almost $360,000 a year, had published a textbook, and was married and the father of two. Hawash's arrest and his subsequent monthlong detention ignited a firestorm of protest in the Pacific Northwest.

"One professor portrayed Hawash's incarceration as 'part of a consistent pattern of suppression of civil liberties.' Columnists and letter writers compared the United States to a 'Third World country,' Orwell's *1984,* Nazi Germany or the Soviet Union. Militant Islamic groups like the Council on American Islamic Relations [CAIR] saw in Hawash's arrest 'serious damage' to the standing of American Muslims." Hawash's friends and his immediate boss denounced the arrest as racial profiling, raised funds for a legal defense fund, set up a FreeMikeHawash.org Web site, and staged protests in the streets of Portland.

What inspired the feds to move against Hawash? Pipes again: Sometime in the year 2000, "Hawash's neighbors began to notice a change in him. He grew a beard, wore Arab clothing, prayed five times a day and regularly attended mosque. He also became noticeably less friendly. . . . Further inquiry found that Hawash paid up his house mortgage (interest payments go against Islamic law) and donated more than $10,000 to the Global Relief Foundation, an Islamic charity subsequently closed for financing terrorist groups. Early in 2001, he went on pilgrimage to Mecca. And 'Middle Eastern males' were seen coming and going from his house."*

Responding to President Bush's call for citizens to be vig-

---

*Daniel Pipes, "The Terrorist Next Door," available at www.danielpipes.org/article/1195.

ilant after 9/11, Hawash's neighbors reported these strange goings-on to the FBI.

Racial profiling? On August 6, 2003, Hawash pleaded guilty to conspiring to help the Taliban and agreed to cooperate fully with the prosecution, including waiving his right to appeal his sentence. That's the kind of plea a defendant cops only when the prosecutors have him dead to rights. And the FBI might never have thought to investigate Hawash if his neighbors had not spoken up.

It's worth remembering incidents like these when you hear complaints about the Bush administration's civil liberties record. In the 2002 State of the Union address, President Bush unveiled an ambitious program that invited American workers to report suspicious activity in public places, especially docks, highways, public transit, and public utilities. These are the sorts of installations that are both most vulnerable to a destructive act of terrorism and also most difficult to police. Here's just one scenario: Ten al-Qaeda men lease ordinary-looking white trucks at ten different locations, load them with explosives, drive one into the middle of the Triborough Bridge, another onto the Golden Gate Bridge, a third to the junction of the Santa Monica and San Diego Freeways, a fourth into the center of the Chicago Loop, and so on, and then, at an appointed hour—detonate them all simultaneously. How in the world do you prevent something like that? Probably the only way would be a tip from the agent who leased one of the trucks—or else maybe a report from a keen-eyed trucker who noticed something untoward about the vehicle in the next lane. That reasonable insight was the genesis of the Terrorist Information and Prevention System, or TIPS for short. To the astonishment of the administration, TIPS provoked an outburst of anger and mockery. Critics conjured up the possibility of deliverymen spying on their customers and meter readers peeking through the windows. The administration responded by issuing new rules that specifically exempted from the program any postal and utility employees who served or even had access to private houses. The revisions failed to mollify, and the final version of the Homeland Security Act that Bush signed in November 2002 forbade the administration to proceed with the idea.

It's curious: Most of the time we praise the alert citizen who identifies and exposes wrongdoing. The actress Julia Roberts won an Academy Award for a role based on the career of Erin Brockovich, a paralegal who accused a utility company of poisoning a community's water. White House counsel John Dean became a national icon a quarter century ago for blowing the whistle on President Nixon. Federal law affirmatively *requires* doctors, nurses, teachers, and day care workers to file a report whenever they suspect that a child has been abused. Yet many of the same people who salute the conscientious citizen who informs the authorities that she suspects a corporation may be poisoning the water would condemn her if she informed them that she suspects her tenant may be plotting to do the same.

This is all wrong. A free society is not an unpoliced society. A free society is a self-policed society. To an extent that often amazes people from other countries, Americans are expected to comply with the laws unsupervised. One reason that so many European countries rely so heavily on sales taxes is that they simply do not trust their people to pay their income taxes. Americans declare their income to the government, estimate their own deductions, and send a check. Americans are often called on to serve on juries. The duty is both irksome and easy to evade—yet by and large it is not evaded, and most of us are mildly scandalized when we hear that a friend or relative has tried to shirk. When we summon to memory the heroes of World War II, we think not only of the fighting men on the front line, but also of the air-raid wardens of the battle of Britain and the good citizens on the home front who donated their aluminum pots and pans to the war effort, went without tires and fresh meat, and invested every spare dollar in war bonds. We have to cast off once and for all the 1970s cynicism that sneered from the back of the classroom at the joiner and volunteer—and reacquire our admiration for the citizen who *does his or her part.*

Most ordinary crimes are solved not by sleuthing, but with information provided to the police. Sometimes the motives of those who provide the information are not very pretty: Maybe they want the reward money, maybe they are seeking revenge for some private wrong, maybe they just never liked the offender, maybe they want him out of the way so that they can woo his girlfriend. Often, however, the motives are admirable: conscience, sympathy for the victim, even a desire to shock a loved one out of a life of crime and into a change of heart.

From the point of view of public safety, however, information from nonsaints can be just as valuable as information from the most conscientious citizen, and this is true whether we are investigating a backstreet mugging or a plot for mass murder. Americans have successfully inculcated in themselves the ideals of tolerance and mutual respect—so successfully that many dozens of articles appeared in newspapers after 9/11 by contributors lashing themselves for casting suspicious glances at the man in Islamic dress on their most recent air flight. This nonsense has to stop. People who live next door to a storefront mosque in Brooklyn, New York, will almost certainly observe more things of interest to counterterrorism officials than will people who live next door to a Christian Science church in Brookline, Massachusetts. The software engineer who develops a sudden enthusiasm for Islam is more likely to be funding terror than the software engineer who develops a sudden enthusiasm for vintage cars.

It would be un-American and stupid to mistrust our neighbors merely because of their names and backgrounds. The Americans of the World War II era were able to distinguish between an Eisenhower, a Wedermeyer, and a Nimitz on the one hand and a Goebbels, a Goering, and a Himmler on the other—and we are at least as capable of drawing distinctions as they were. From the Arabic speakers who translate intercepts for the National Security Agency (NSA) to the brave agents who have tried to infiltrate al-Qaeda cells; from the Afghan American taxi drivers who return home to open businesses in Kabul to intellectuals and artists like Fouad Ajami and Salman Rushdie who uphold the ideals of freedom and pluralism often at the risk of their lives—all in all, many of the most valiant and effective fighters against Islamic extremism have been men and women of Muslim faith and origin themselves. That should never be forgotten.

But neither should it be forgotten that the terrorist thrives in obscurity and inattention. Scrutiny is his deadliest enemy.

There has been much debate since 9/11 about the need for "profiling" to catch potential terrorists without forcing law-abiding travelers to stand in long lines. In our view, ethnic profiling—looking for people with Muslim-sounding names or Middle Eastern facial features—is a divisive and humiliating waste of time. As the cases of Johnny Walker Lindh, Richard Reid, and José Padilla demonstrate, Islamic terrorists can be born in any country and can belong to any race. Nor should we exclude the possibility that Islamic terrorism may begin to make common cause with Western political extremists of the far Left and the far Right. In 2002, Holland's most outspoken critic of militant Islam, Pim Fortuyn, was murdered not by a Muslim, but by a left-wing activist who (according to his own testimony) regarded Fortuyn as a "considerable danger to the weaker groups in society," which were, as the killer defined them, Muslims, asylum seekers, immigrants, and animals. Just as the communists were once aided by fellow travelers who endorsed their program and condoned their crimes, so Islamic extremists may find fellow travelers in the non-Muslim West. Indeed, they are already finding them. David Frum stood under the dome of St. Paul's Cathedral on Easter Monday 2003 and heard a minister of the Church of England preach a sermon extolling Rachel Corrie as a model of Christian courage and self-sacrifice: Corrie was the young American who was accidentally buried under a collapsing pile of dirt as she tried to block an Israeli bulldozer from excavating tunnels used to smuggle arms and explosives into Israel from Gaza. (Eleven days after Corrie's death, the Israeli Defense Forces arrested an armed Islamic Jihad terrorist in the Jenin offices of Corrie's group, the International Solidarity Movement. ISM also hosted the British suicide bomber Asif Mohammed Hanif and his co-conspirator Omar Khan Sharif only five days before they killed three people and wounded fifty in an April 30, 2003, suicide attack on a Tel Aviv nightclub.)

What investigators need to profile is not *ethnicity*—it is *behavior*. Imagine this scenario, for example: An individual travels by air from an urban center to a rural town. He checks into a motel. He purchases a quantity of agricultural chemicals. He rents a van. He drives to another urban area, rents a storage locker, and returns the van. Then he travels by bus to New York City. Weeks later he removes the contents of the storage locker, rents another van, and drives toward New York. Yes, it is certainly possible that this individual might be an eccentric New Yorker trying to grow a lawn on the roof of his Chicago town house, who takes advantage of a visit to his cousin in Bucks County to buy chemicals at Cousin Joe's feed store. But wouldn't we like to know just a little bit more about him before we decided he was harmless?

There are new surveillance techniques that make it possible to monitor behavior indicative of terrorism without compromising the privacy of the individuals engaged in the behavior if they should later prove to be innocent. New data assembly techniques can pull together inside a computer an individual's credit history, his recent movements, his immigration status and personal background, his age and sex, and a hundred other pieces of information and present them to the analyst—*without the analyst or any other human being ever knowing the individual's identity.* The dossier of data would be assigned a case number, and stringent internal codes and controls would hermetically segregate the dossier's number from the name of the person to whom the dossier referred. Only if the dossier gave probable cause to investigate further would investigators seek a warrant to permit the name and the data to be joined together, and then to authorize further surveillance. This is profiling as it ought to be done: not an excuse for discrimination, but an attempt to concentrate scarce police resources at points of greatest danger.

Denying Terrorists Material and Moral Support

ALTHOUGH ISLAMIC TERRORISM originated overseas, it seems to be drawing crucial—and increasing—support from a growing infrastructure of extremism inside this country and in Canada.

Immediately after the 9/11 attacks, the Bush administration went searching for Muslim American leaders willing to condemn al-Qaeda's crime in vigorous and unequivocal terms. Disturbingly, many of the most prominent figures in the organized Muslim American community were either unwilling to speak forthrightly or were tainted by extremist associations of their own—or both. In the end, the White House found a mild-mannered and apparently apolitical California imam, Muzamil Siddiqi. Yet even Siddiqi had a blemish on his record: When asked by the *Los Angeles Times* in 1989 whether he approved or disapproved of the Ayatollah Khomeini's fatwa against Salman Rushdie, Siddiqi had declined to condemn it.

At least Siddiqi had never actually endorsed violence. There are all too many American Muslim leaders of whom that cannot be said. In June 2002, a spokesman for FBI director Robert Mueller described the American Muslim Council (AMC) as "the most mainstream Muslim group in the country." Yet at a demonstration in Lafayette Park on October 28, 2000, the AMC's founder, Abdurahman Alamoudi, offered this account of his political beliefs: "I have been labeled by the media in New York to be a supporter of Hamas. Anybody support Hamas here?" When the crowd of three thousand screamed approval, he repeated the question and continued: "Hear that, Bill Clinton? We are all supporters of Hamas. I wish they added that I am also a supporter of Hezbollah." (In October 2003, Alamoudi was indicted on charges of illegally accepting $340,000 from the government of Libya for his efforts to persuade the U.S. government to lift sanctions imposed on Libya for its support of terrorism.)

Alamoudi's successor as executive director of the AMC,

Eric Vickers, exulted over the destruction of the space shuttle *Columbia* in a February 2003 e-mail to supporters:

> "The Book of Revelations," she said in pointing to her Bible, "tells of the things to come and the signs to watch for." This was the sum and substance of a conversation I happened to have with a fellow passenger on a plane ride the night before the spaceship *Columbia* disintegrated before the eyes of the world.
>
> I have been tempted to contact her to ask if she sees a sign in the calamitous destruction of the one hundred and thirteenth space shuttle mission taking place over a city named Palestine, while on board was the first Israeli astronaut, who also happened to have been the pilot that bombed several years ago an Iraqi nuclear facility.*

The Council on American Islamic Relations, probably the most media savvy of American Muslim groups, declared its opposition to the Afghan campaign as early as October 2001. CAIR has condemned all the administration's antiterrorism legislation and cosponsored anti–Iraq war demonstrations with the far left group ANSWER. CAIR continued to raise funds for and defend the former H. Rap Brown (now a convert to Islam) even after his conviction for the murder of an Atlanta policeman—despite Brown's long history of violence and extremism, including his public threat to murder Lady Bird Johnson while she was First Lady of the United States.

Trailing only slightly behind CAIR in the Nexis sweep-

* www.house.gov/nadler/AMC_020503.htm.

stakes is the Muslim Public Affairs Council. On the very day of 9/11, the group's executive director, Salam al-Marayati, gave an interview to a Los Angeles radio station in which he said that the state of Israel belonged on the list of possible culprits.

The militancy of the Muslim American lobby groups echoes what is being said inside the nation's mosques. The Cleveland Islamic Center is one of the largest mosques in the nation. Its imam, Fawaz Damra, a prominent citizen of the city, presided over multifaith events after the 9/11 attacks. But ten years before 9/11, Damra, a newly arrived Palestinian, was caught on videotape raising money in Chicago for Islamic Jihad: The "Jihad stabs Jews. Twelve Jews . . . Who will give $500?" The money he sought would direct "a rifle at the first and last enemy of the Islamic nation, and that is the sons of monkeys and pigs, the Jews." When confronted with the stab-the-Jews tape in 2001, Damra issued a written apology—and then in an in-person interview suggested that he was the victim of a Jewish conspiracy to marginalize Islam. Somebody, he said, decided about him that "this is a moderate voice for Islam, and he is getting too much powerful. He will make America see the real Islam. And they decided, no!"*

In the same month in which Damra's history was revealed, the imam of what may be the nation's wealthiest and most prestigious mosque, on Manhattan's East 96th Street,

* Hanna Rosin, "Mosque Leader's Past Returns to Haunt Him; Jews Describe Overtures as 'Trojan Horse,' " *The Washington Post*, October 29, 2001, p. A3.

decamped to his native Egypt and gave an interview in which
he asserted that after 9/11, Muslims were murdered in the
streets of New York and poisoned by Jewish doctors in the
city's hospitals. He alleged that his own home had been attacked by an angry mob. "I went out to them and asked why
they were doing this. . . . During my conversations with this
group, it became clear to me that they knew very well that the
Jews were behind these ugly acts." He then repeated the fantasy that four thousand New York Jews had received word to
stay home from work that day.*

Extremist attitudes like these are not nearly as unusual
among the leaders of American mosques as they ought to be.
In a speech to the State Department in January 1999, Hisham
Kabbani, the leader of the American branch of Sufi Islam and
a nephew of a former grand mufti of Lebanon, warned that
80 percent of the two thousand or so mosques in America
were run by leaders of "extremist ideologies." Extremism
was enforced through the granting or withholding of funds.
Most mosques are fairly poor and rely heavily on gifts of
money from umbrella groups like the Islamic Society of
North America. That money, in turn, tends to originate with
practitioners of Saudi-style Wahhabi Islam in this country
and abroad—that is, when it does not come from the government of Saudi Arabia itself.

Extremist Muslim leaders then try to inculcate extremist
beliefs in the students at the nation's estimated three hundred

---

* The imam's name is Muhammed al-Gamei'a, and an English translation of the full
text of his interview can be read at www.memri.org/bin/articles.cgi?Page=archives&
Area=sd&ID=SP28801.

to six hundred Muslim day schools. *The Washington Post* reported in March 2002:

> Eleventh-graders at the elite Islamic Saudi Academy in Northern Virginia study energy and matter in physics, write out differential equations in precalculus and read stories about slavery and the Puritans in English. Then they file into their Islamic studies class, where the textbooks tell them the Day of Judgment can't come until Jesus Christ returns to Earth, breaks the cross and converts everyone to Islam, and until Muslims start attacking Jews.
>
> The 11th-grade textbook, for example, says one sign of the Day of Judgment will be that Muslims will fight and kill Jews, who will hide behind trees that say: "Oh Muslim, Oh servant of God, here is a Jew hiding behind me. Come here and kill him." Several students of different ages [at the academy], all of whom asked not to be identified, said that in Islamic studies, they are taught that it is better to shun and even to dislike Christians, Jews and Shi'ite Muslims. Some teachers "focus more on hatred," said one teenager, who recited by memory the signs of the coming of the Day of Judgment. "They teach students that whatever is kuffar [non-Muslim], it is okay for you" to hurt or steal from that person.

The Islamic studies class at Washington Islamic Academy in Springfield, Virginia (the town in which Ziad Jarrah falsely claimed to live when he applied for his Virginia driver's license), uses a Pakistani textbook that describes Christian beliefs as "nonsense" and portrays Jews as treacherous people who financially "oppress" others. The school's Islamic studies teacher claims never to show those pages to her students. But on the maps of the world that hang in the school's classrooms, the word *Israel* "is blackened out with marker, with 'Palestine' written in its place." A teacher at the Islamic Academy's school for girls expressed doubts to the *Post* about whether Osama bin Laden was truly responsible for the 9/11 attacks. She "wonders whether the United States just needed someone to blame and picked a Muslim. 'A lot of the students can't make up their minds if [bin Laden] is a good guy or a bad guy,' [the teacher] said. 'There are some Muslims who think he did it and others who don't. The thing is, we don't have any real proof either way. I think a lot of people feel this way.' "*

Similarly, American Muslim groups vigorously defended nine U.S. citizens and two aliens arrested on gun and conspiracy charges for training with Kashmiri terrorists to wage jihad against U.S. troops in Afghanistan and elsewhere. (Three of the men pleaded guilty in August 2003; the rest were awaiting trial as this book went to press.) The arrested men's attorney acknowledged that "deciding to go to the Lashkar-i-Taiba training camp was a terrible mistake" but pointed out that they "never participated in a terrorist attack."† Of course, the main reason they never participated in an attack may have been that they were caught in time. Not so an Egyptian-born immigrant, devout Muslim, and permanent American resident named Hesham Mohamed Hadayet, who walked toward the El Al ticket counter at Los Angeles

---

* Valerie Strauss and Emily Wax, "Where Two Worlds Collide; Muslim Schools Face Tension of Islamic, U.S. Views," *The Washington Post*, February 25, 2002, p. A1.

† Jerry Markon, "Three Plead Guilty in Jihad Conspiracy," *The Washington Post*, August 26, 2003, p. A1.

International Airport on July 4, 2002, pulled out two pistols, and began blasting. Hadayet meant to kill on a large scale. He was carrying a spare magazine for each gun in his shirt pockets; he had also armed himself with a six-inch hunting knife. In the event, he killed two people and wounded another in the time it took two heroic El Al guards, who were themselves both seriously wounded, to tackle and kill him. When police arrived at Hadayet's apartment in Irvine, the first thing they saw was a sticker on his door: "Read the Koran." At the time of the writing of this book, Hadayet's apparently spontaneous act was the most recent terrorist murder on U.S. soil.

It remains a very rare event for native-born American Muslims to participate in acts of terror. Militant Islam in the United States expresses itself primarily through lobbying and fund-raising. As early as 1995, federal investigators alerted the Clinton White House that one of the largest Muslim charities in the United States, the Holy Land Foundation of Richardson, Texas, was directing millions to Hamas and Islamic Jihad. The authorities hesitated to act for six years, during which time the foundation grew to a $10-million-a-year operation. Not until December 2001 did President Bush at last close the Holy Land Foundation. After even more years of hesitation, the government of Canada closed one of the largest Muslim charities north of the border, the Benevolence International Foundation, in late 2002.

Even now, however, we know troublingly little about the finances of terrorism. We do not know how much terrorists and extremists raise in North America through direct appeals that bypass organized charity. In January 2003, German police arrested a Yemeni cleric, Sheikh Mohammed Ali Hassan al-Moayad, who claimed to have raised $20 million for Osama bin Laden before 9/11, much of it from inside the United States. Nor do we know how much terrorists and extremists rake off from the informal money transmission services that send unrecorded sums from legal and illegal immigrant communities in North America back home to the Middle East and South Asia. In 2001, the Bush administration shut down one of these services, al-Barakaat of Somalia, but there are others, and they remain as vulnerable to abuse as ever. Nor do we know how much they earn from crime and fraud. Hezbollah seems to have earned millions selling pirated compact discs in South America. A Hezbollah ring in Charlotte, North Carolina, raised funds to buy advanced military hardware and software by smuggling truckloads of contraband cigarettes into high-tax Michigan.* A man described as Osama bin Laden's "European ambassador," a Palestinian imam named Omar Mohammed Othman, entered Britain as a refugee in 1991 (he claimed to be a victim of religious persecution after a Jordanian court sentenced him to death for a series of bomb attacks, one of which killed a twelve-year-old girl). Over the next ten years, he received subsidized housing and a welfare payment of some 213 pounds a month. The British authorities stopped his benefit after a February 2001

---

* Steve Emerson, *American Jihad: The Terrorists Living Among Us* (Free Press, 2002), pp. 35–36.

police raid on his house found almost a quarter of a million dollars in Spanish pesetas, German marks, British pounds, and American currency. How much of this kind of activity continues today? We must despairingly conclude: Nobody knows—nobody other than the terrorists themselves, that is.

We can get at the flow of money from North America to terror by cracking down not only on terror-tainted charities, but on the charities' donors. Donating money to a terrorist group has been a crime in the United States since 1995; we need to underscore the seriousness of this prohibition with some dramatic prosecutions and exemplary sentences.

We should strike too at incitement to terror in schools and mosques. Since 1970, the IRS has denied tax exemptions to schools that practice racial segregation. Schools that inculcate violence should equally be denied this privilege. The Saudi Islamic Academy may have a First Amendment right to diffuse fantasies of anti-Semitic slaughter—but it is far-fetched to suppose that it has a right to issue tax deductions or avoid property taxes as it does so. As for mosques, the IRS has over the years adopted regulations that define what is and what is not a bona fide religious institution. If those regulations cannot now be interpreted to exclude buildings in which murder is preached, they should be revised—and fast.

Individuals who endorse or condone terrorism should obviously never be welcome at the White House, or indeed any office of the U.S. government. The same commonsense rule should extend to groups that employ such individuals as officers or have them on their boards of directors. Until the

American Muslim Council, the Council on American Islamic Relations, and the Muslim Public Affairs Council purge themselves of their extremists, they should be regarded as fellow travelers of the terrorist enemy and treated with appropriate mistrust and disdain by Congress and the executive branch.

A second Patriot Act was proposed and abandoned in 2002, but at least one of the ideas in it remains valuable and necessary. Under existing law, an American citizen can be deemed to have renounced his citizenship if he joins a foreign army. The now discarded Patriot Act II would have extended this principle to foreign terrorist organizations: When an American citizen joins al-Qaeda, that decision should have consequences at least as severe as the decision to enlist in the Royal Air Force or the Bundeswehr.

But all of this is just a beginning. Important as it is for law enforcement to crack down on actual lawbreaking and for Congress to kick away the financial props under terror-tainted organizations, extremism in the American Muslim community is much more than a legal or even a security problem. It is a moral challenge for all Americans, Muslim and non-Muslim. Another story from Daniel Pipes: In 1995, members of the bin Laden family and others with known terrorist connections established a small "Islamic" bank, BMI Inc., in New Jersey. In 1999, a BMI employee tipped off the FBI that BMI funds may have financed the East Africa embassy bombings. The president of the bank got wind of the tip and hurriedly called the FBI to ask for a meeting. The assistant U.S. attorney dealing with the case urged FBI agent Gamal Abdel-Hafiz, a naturalized American Muslim, to wear a wire to the meeting. The agent refused and in the hearing of three witnesses explained that as a Muslim, he could not record the words of another Muslim. Abdel-Hafiz also refused to record a conversation with Sami al-Arian, the now indicted Islamic Jihad leader from the University of South Florida; in that instance too he cited his feelings of religious solidarity. Now the punch line: When one of Abdel-Hafiz's fellow agents complained to FBI headquarters, officials there shrugged off the complaint. "You have to understand where he's coming from," a superior told the complaining agent. In February 2001, Abdel-Hafiz, the FBI agent who would not spy on Muslims, was promoted to a highly sensitive and prestigious post in . . . Saudi Arabia!* (In the summer of 2003, Abdel-Hafiz was removed from his post and put on administrative leave.)

The lax multiculturalism that urges Americans to accept the unacceptable from their fellow citizens is one of this nation's greatest vulnerabilities in the war on terror. American society must communicate to its Muslim citizens and residents a clear message about what is expected from them. The flow of funds to terror must stop. The incitement in schools and mosques must stop. The promotion of anti-Semitism must stop. The denial and excuse-making must stop. Community leaders should cooperate wholeheartedly with law en-

* Daniel Pipes, "The FBI Fumbles," available at www.danielpipes.org/article/1038.

forcement to identify and monitor potentially dangerous people, and Muslim leaders should abjure violence and terror without reservation or purpose of evasion.

At the same time, we should honor moderate and patriotic Islam as an important and respected element of American life. We urgently need an American Islam that feels at home on American soil, that is committed to American values and the defense of the American nation. If you listen carefully, you can hear that American Islam struggling to be born—in, for example, essays like this, by Sheila Musaji, editor of the on-line magazine *The American Muslim*:

> I had noticed over the past few years that many of the individuals who had represented the Islamic 'middle path' and a moderate voice in the public dialogue on Islam—who stood for justice (for Muslims and non-Muslims)—who spoke for dialogue, peace, tolerance, building bridges (within the community and with other communities), changing hearts by example as opposed to argumentative preaching,—who spoke up against intolerance, violence and injustice (against Muslims or non-Muslims, whether carried out by Muslims or non-Muslims)—who saw themselves as proud Muslims and proud Americans—had faded from the pages of the Muslim media, had vanished one by one from our local mosque, had been replaced by other voices that promoted a vision of Islam that promotes anger, discord and even violence.*

The struggle for an American Islam has only just begun. On issues from women's rights to free inquiry, religious toler-

---

* theamericanmuslim.org/about.htm.

ance, and loyalty in time of war, American Muslims have tough decisions to make about how to adjust old ways to new ideals. But the power of those American ideals is very great— and their truth is compelling. Who knows but that the force that ultimately defeats and destroys militant Islam may not turn out to be a democratic Islam born in the United States?

5. THE WAR ABROAD

"EVERYTHING IS VERY simple in war, but the simplest thing is difficult": So Karl von Clausewitz warned two hundred years ago, and it remains true today. The things we need to do to win the war on terror are simple, but they will not be easy.

We must cut off the terrorists' access to weapons of mass destruction.

We must deny them money and refuge.

We must hunt down the individual terrorists before they kill our people or others.

We must destroy regimes implicated in anti-American terrorism.

We must deter *all* regimes that use terror as a weapon of state against anyone, American or not.

And, ultimately, we must discredit and defeat the extremist Islamic ideology that justifies and sustains terrorism.

First, foremost, and fastest, we have to deal with the interrelated nuclear programs of Iran and North Korea. The world's first Islamic republic and the world's last Stalinist autocracy have been cooperating for years on nuclear bomb making, with occasional paid assists from Pakistan. North Korea claims already to possess some bombs; Iran is very close—perhaps three years away, in the optimistic view of U.S. intelligence, maybe twelve to eighteen months, by the less sanguine Israeli estimate.

Iran is itself a terrorist state, the world's worst. North Korea has committed terrorist atrocities, too: In 1983, a bomb planted by a North Korean terror team murdered seventeen top South Korean officials. Both regimes are nightmarishly repressive; both regimes present intolerable threats to American security. We must move boldly against them both and against all the other sponsors of terrorism as well: Syria, Libya, and Saudi Arabia. And we don't have much time.

North Korea

IT'S OFTEN SAID that all our options in North Korea are bad ones. But having only bad options against an imminent nuclear threat is like offering a starving man only bad food: One still must choose *something*.

Our options are poor because the North Koreans can credibly threaten to inflict terrible damage on South Korea even without a nuclear bomb. The South Korean capital, Seoul, lies less than twenty-four miles from the armistice line with the North. In the hills along that line, the North Koreans have concealed thousands of artillery tubes and rocket launchers. These tubes would not last long in a war against the South: At the second a tube or launcher fired, its place would be marked by American reconnaissance, and American and South Korean missiles or planes would swiftly destroy it. But the sheer number of tubes and launchers emplaced means that a North Korean barrage would continue for many hours, perhaps even some days.

We have no doubt how such a war would end: The North Korean regular armed forces, though numerous, are poorly equipped, and even their supposedly elite units would not survive long under skies controlled by American airpower. But the fear of the damage from that opening barrage understandably terrifies the South Koreans, and that terror has tragically divided their interests from ours. The South Koreans, to speak plainly, favor a policy of appeasement of the North. As for the risk from the North's nuclear weapons, it does not worry the South Koreans overmuch, because they believe that the North would not use the bomb against *them.* Accordingly, the top priority of South Korea's current government has been to ensure that the United States and Japan join them in appeasing Kim Jong Il. To that end, they wish to keep as many American troops as possible deployed as far forward as possible, so that Americans share their vulnerability to North Korean artillery.

However, our interests (and those of Japan) differ from those of South Korea. Put bluntly: A North Korean nuclear warhead that might be sold to al-Qaeda or some other terrorist group is more dangerous to us than a war on the Korean peninsula. Many Japanese officials feel the same way, and even more strongly, for their cities lie within range of North Korean missiles while ours do not, not yet. And the Japanese people have perhaps a grimmer awareness of the horrors of the North Korean system than we do: In the 1970s and 1980s, North Korean agents kidnapped at least thirteen Japanese citizens to teach Japanese at North Korean spy schools; only five of these prisoners remain alive.

In Korea, the surest way to avoid war is to prepare to fight it. The key to the North Korean problem may well be China. Although the United States is the largest source of foreign aid to the hungry people of North Korea, it is China that sustains the North Korean government and military. It matters little that the Chinese leadership dislikes and distrusts Kim Jong Il. China provides the coal that keeps the North Korean arms industry running; the fuel for North Korea's missiles; the fertilizer that grows the food eaten by North Korean soldiers; and North Korea's only outlets to the world that cannot be closed by American, Japanese, and South Korean air and naval power. It is via China too that Kim Jong Il would have to make his escape if war actually did break out.

The leaders of China appreciate, perhaps even better than we do, that a second Korean war would end with the destruction of the North Korean regime, the unification of the whole peninsula under a democratic government in Seoul, and an unfriendly army deployed on China's borders. China went to war in 1950 to prevent such an outcome. If China wants to avoid unification today, it will have to use its influence on its client to *prevent* war.

The Bush administration, like the Clinton administration before it, has pressed China to use that influence. At the same time, and again like the Clinton administration, the Bush administration has attempted to work multilaterally to stop the export to North Korea of the technology necessary to complete a bomb. Unlike the Clinton administration, the Bush administration has refused to offer the North Koreans bribes to drop their nuclear program, but people can be found within the administration who would readily revert to that policy, too. Such people agree with Madeleine Albright, who argues in her memoir, "The way out [of the Korean problem] in 2003 does not differ much from the way out in 1994":* bribery.

But "the way out" that the Clinton administration pursued in 1994 was premised on a double fraud: North Korea deceived us because first we deceived ourselves. We paid North Korea hundreds of millions of dollars in aid—we even agreed to supply them with two nuclear power plants—if only they would relinquish their nuclear weapons and missile programs. Was it ever plausible that Kim Jong Il would keep his word? He signed, then cheated. When caught cheating, he reneged. If he signs another agreement today, he will renege on it, too. Lionel Trilling famously said that human beings have a moral duty to be intelligent. We would add that the makers of foreign policy have a moral duty not to be gullible. The Clinton "pay the North Koreans to be nice" approach has produced an utter and obvious debacle. It is time for stronger medicine.

---

* Madeleine Albright, *Madame Secretary: A Memoir* (Miramax, 2003), p. 471.

Any new agreement with the North Koreans must begin by acknowledging that North Korea cannot be trusted to honor its promises. The test of the value of future agreements is simply this: Can they be verified without relying on the worthless declarations of the North Koreans themselves? We would propose a four-point checklist.

First, no agreement is worth having if it does not provide for the immediate surrender by North Korea of all the nuclear material they are known to possess *before* North Korea receives a single dollar in new American aid: not a phased surrender, not an incremental surrender, but a total and complete surrender. The United States should be willing to compensate a former nuclear state for the loss of its nuclear arsenal—but should never pay what could be described as blackmail to an existing nuclear state.

Second, North Korea must close its missile bases. Unlike nuclear plants, missile bases can be observed from the air, so U.S. satellites can verify whether North Korea has made good on its commitment.

Third, North Korea must submit to the permanent presence of an International Atomic Energy Agency inspection team, but a team that operates by stringent new rules. The inspectors must be based in North Korea, must be allowed to go anywhere at any time, and must be allowed to remove North Korean nuclear scientists and their families to neutral territory and interview them there.

On those terms, the United States can probably live with the risks of North Korean cheating, and U.S. diplomats will have done a good day's work if they could persuade North Korea to accept them. But we fear that it is unlikely that North Korea will accept such terms. We fear that the North Korean leadership craves a nuclear arsenal even more desperately than it hungers for international approval or American aid. If those fears are correct, then the United States must ready itself for the hard possibility that our choices really shrink to two: tolerate North Korea's attempt to go nuclear— or take decisive action to stop it.

Decisive action would begin with a comprehensive air and naval blockade of North Korea, cutting it off from all seaborne traffic, all international aviation, and all intercourse with the South. South Korea will object, but it needs to be made to understand that, as in Cuba in 1962, a blockade is its best alternative to war. Of course, North Korea's land border with China will remain open. That's good. It underscores our central contention, that the North Korean nuclear program is a Chinese responsibility, for which China will be held accountable.

Next, we must accelerate the redeployment of our ground troops on the Korean peninsula so they are beyond the range of North Korean artillery and short-range rockets. President Bush and Secretary Rumsfeld have already begun to do this. U.S. troops originally served to deter the North from invading a second time; today they have become hostages, whose vulnerability the *North* exploits to deter *us*—and whose presence discourages the South from improving its own defenses.

Third, as we reposition troops, we should develop detailed plans for a preemptive strike against North Korea's nuclear facilities. Of course, it is true that we do not know where all these facilities are. But we know where the most important one is; and just as a surgeon will wish to remove a malignant tumor even if he suspects that there may be others that cannot be located, so we should not hesitate to hit the bomb factory we can find, even if other facilities may be hidden underground.

But we hope—and this hope is, we think, well founded—that a credible buildup to an American strike will persuade the Chinese finally to do what they have so often promised to do: bring the North Koreans to heel. In return, the Chinese get peace on their frontiers and a North Korean government friendly to them. It may be that the only way out of the decade-long crisis on the Korean peninsula is the toppling of Kim Jong Il and his replacement by a North Korean communist who is *more* subservient to China. If so, we should accept that outcome. However menacing China may become over the long term, it is much more sane and predictable than communist North Korea has been. And a more pro-Chinese North Korea would also probably institute more rational economic policies, thereby saving millions of North Korean people from famine and misery.

In time, all of Korea will be united in liberty. Eventual Korean unification will reinforce the power of the world's democracies against an aggressive and undemocratic China, should China so evolve. But that is tomorrow's challenge. For today, it will be more than enough to force North Korea to eschew nuclear blackmail.

Iran

IRAN WANTS A lot more than blackmail from us—and so poses a much larger danger than North Korea. The mullahs of Iran are sheltering part of the surviving leadership of al-Qaeda. They created and supported Hezbollah, the terror group that killed almost three hundred American soldiers and civilians in Lebanon and Spain in 1983 and 1984 (and, *n'ou-bliez pas,* fifty-eight French soldiers as well). Since 1979, Iran has sponsored the murder of some eighty exiled Iranian dissidents, including one on American soil: Ali Akbar Tabatabai, leader of the Iran Freedom Foundation and a prominent critic of the Khomeini regime, assassinated at his home in Bethesda, Maryland, by an American convert to Islam originally named David Belfield. Under his new name of Daoud Salahuddin, Belfield is sheltered by Iran to this day.

Iran almost certainly directed the murder of Iraq's most prominent pro-American Shiite cleric, Abdul Majid al-Khoei, within days of his return from twelve years of exile to his home in Najaf. Iran foments Palestinian terrorism against Israel, using terror to undermine every attempt to encourage an Israeli-Palestinian peace. Iran was also responsible for the single worst anti-Semitic atrocity in the history of the Western Hemisphere, the bombing of the Jewish Community Center in Buenos Aires in 1994, a crime that killed eighty-six people and wounded two hundred others—and that followed another presumed Iranian atrocity, the 1992 bombing of the Israeli embassy in Buenos Aires, which killed twenty-nine. Perhaps most ominous of all, Iran's mullahs are recklessly goading Israel in a manner that could explode into a larger regional conflict. In a December 2001 sermon, Iran's second most powerful figure, Akbar Hashemi Rafsanjani, declared that Israel was "the most hideous historic occurrence in history," which the Islamic world "will vomit out from its midst" through nuclear warfare. Rafsanjani promised that an Islamic republic would soon have nuclear weapons. "On that day, the strategy of the West will hit a dead end, since a single atomic bomb has the power to completely destroy Israel, while an Israeli counterstrike can only cause partial damage to the Islamic world."* Threats like these almost compel Israel to strike Iran's nuclear facilities preemptively—with unforeseeable consequences for all.

In his speech to Congress on September 20, 2001, President Bush declared, "From this day forward, any nation that continues to harbor or support terrorism will be regarded by the United States as a hostile regime." Iran continues to harbor and support terrorism, and its hostility does not have to be inferred: It is declared and manifest. Yet many of our leaders continue to insist that we can and should do business with "moderates" in the leadership of Iran. In February 2002, Deputy Secretary of State Richard Armitage made the incredible statement that he considered Iran to be a "democracy."† Meanwhile, our Euro-

---

* Jack Katzenell, "Peres Protests Iranian Threat to Destroy Israel," Associated Press Worldstream, December 25, 2001.

† "The axis of evil was a valid comment, [but] I would note there's one dramatic difference between Iran and the other two axes of evil, and that would be its democracy. [And] you approach a democracy differently. I wouldn't think they [Iran] were next at all." Quoted in Robin Wright, "U.S. Now Views Iran in More Favorable Light," Los Angeles Times, February 14, 2003, p. 5.

pean allies press us to rely on multilateral diplomacy to halt the Iranian bomb program, notwithstanding that this diplomacy has failed and failed again for more than a decade.

Those of us who advocate a firm foreign policy are often accused of letting ideology prevail over common sense. But if ever there was an example of ideology running roughshod over the facts, it is the delusional approach that our soft-liners have taken to Iran.

Iran a democracy? Well, it has an elected parliament and president—but then, so does North Korea. Nobody can run for office in Iran unless he has been approved by the religious oligarchy that truly rules the country. It is the mullahs who control the army, the secret police, and the courts. They can disallow any law passed by the legislature. They approve every candidate for office. In the 1997 election that brought Mohammed Khatami to power, two hundred people applied for permission to run and only four got it—and three of them were clerics. As one observer quipped, the election offered the Iranian people a choice between "a fanatical fundamentalist, a really fanatical fundamentalist and a really, really fanatical fundamentalist." No surprise that the merely fanatical candidate won—but no worries for the regime, either: Under Iran's Islamic constitution, if the president at any point shows himself insufficiently fanatical, he can be dismissed by the mullahs. Much of the country's wealth passes through the clergy's hands; and in fact it is the growing gap between the vast wealth of the clergy and the plunging living standards of the vast majority of the Iranian population (income per capita has dropped by 25 percent over the past twenty-five years)* that is pushing the country to the brink of revolution.

Moderates in the leadership? Like who? Like President Khatami? One of Khatami's most loyal supporters in the Iranian legislature is Ali Akbar Mohtashemi, a founder of Hezbollah and one of the key planners of the 1983 marine barracks bombing. How moderate can a leadership be when it holds more journalists in jail than any country in the world? Where satellite dishes are illegal and where the state bans all private Internet service providers?

And as for the idea that multilateral agreements can somehow restrain the Iranian nuclear program? Forget it. These agreements actually *encourage* nuclear proliferation. Here's how they work: In 1970, Iran signed the Nuclear Non-proliferation Treaty (NPT). That commitment conferred on Iran the right to import nuclear technology and nuclear materials for "peaceful" purposes. In return, Iran must submit to inspections by the International Atomic Energy Agency. But under existing treaties, the IAEA is permitted to inspect only those nuclear sites Iran declares available for inspection. Even the supposedly stricter regime to which the Iranians agreed in October 2003 does not alter the basic grammar of the IAEA. Under the new deal, Iran has promised to suspend its nearly completed uranium-enrichment program and allow inspectors to visit more places within the country on shorter notice. But the program Iran is now suspending is one that

---

* Measured in 1995 U.S. dollars, Iran's GDP per capita was $2,137 in 1977 and $1,649 in the year 2000, according to the World Bank.

for years it denied possessing. We learned of it only because a brave band of Iranian dissidents risked their lives to reveal it to the world in August 2002.

All those nonproliferation treaties in which soft-liners put so much faith are based on the assumption that we can trust the world's least trustworthy regime to tell us its deepest secrets. Over the past twenty years, the IAEA has been surprised and surprised and surprised again: by India, by Iraq,* by Pakistan, and by North Korea. After a February 2003 inspection tour of Iran, an IAEA spokesman acknowledged that the agency had been surprised once again: "We knew that Iran was working on a centrifuge program. But we were surprised by the number of centrifuge pieces waiting to be assembled. They had a hundred-plus centrifuges built, and they were building more." The Iranians had other surprises for the IAEA, too: They forbade them to visit the facility that many believed to be the headquarters of the centrifuge program. And shortly after the IAEA inspectors left Iran, Iranian dissidents revealed—and satellite photography confirmed—two additional nuclear sites of which the IAEA had been entirely unaware.

Iran's formal adherence to the NPT actually makes it much harder to take effective action to curtail Iran's obvious intentions to acquire nuclear weapons. In fact, the only real restraint imposed by antiproliferation agreements is the restraint on the rest of the world, which is obliged to pretend to believe the most glaring lies.

* Iraq used its membership in the IAEA, and its nationals assigned to work there, to learn the agency's inspection methods and techniques, the better to foil them.

We do not think it is "common sense" to pretend to believe what is manifestly untrue. The mullahs are pursuing a bomb. Our idea of common sense is to stop them.

Here's more common sense: On the basis of our present information, we are not going to be able to stop them by bombing their nuclear facilities. The Iranians have learned a lesson from Israeli's 1981 destruction of Iraq's Osirak reactor and have scattered their nuclear program through their huge country, which is twice the size of Texas. In any event, the problem in Iran is much bigger than the weapons. The problem is the terrorist regime that seeks the weapons. The regime must go.

That is not merely the opinion of the authors of this book. It is the opinion of the vast majority of the Iranian people. Since 1999, the streets of Iran have been filling up with bigger and bigger demonstrations by students, workers, and ordinary people who want the freedom to watch television, to wear lipstick, to choose their own clothes; who want jobs and opportunity; and above all who want a voice in their own government. The demonstrations in the summer of 2003 were the most massive yet. How did those protesters protest? They chanted slogans like "Death to the Taliban in Kabul and Teheran." And they waved American flags. The regime's response was brutal but ineffectual. Protesters reported that they heard the regime's goons speaking to one another in Arabic rather than Persian—apparently the mullahs no longer trust Iranians to do their killing for them.

Would it somehow discredit the protesters in Iranian nationalist eyes (as some in our State Department contend) if the United States were to offer them aid? For an answer, listen to the words of just one dissident, who fled Iran for American-ruled Iraq in the summer of 2003: Iran, he said, is "the world's worst dictatorship." It must be transformed into a "democratic regime that does not make use of religion as a means of oppressing the people and strangling society." Iran, this dissident said, stands on the verge of "popular revolution." How would he feel about American help, including possibly even military assistance? "Freedom is more important than bread. If the Americans will provide it, let them come." Who is this advocate of secularism, democracy, and Iranian-American friendship? Hussein Khomeini, the grandson of Ayatollah Khomeini.*

Khomeini's opposition to the ruling regime echoes that of four of the country's supreme religious authorities, the ayatollahs Hussein Ali Montazeri, Sadiq Ruhani, Yousuf Sani'i, and Muhaqiq Damad.

The Iranian dissidents of 2003 need from us the same thing that Polish dissidents needed back in the 1980s. They need communications equipment, so that dissidents in the country can transmit accurate information out—and so that dissidents inside the country can then broadcast the news back inside. They need money to support the families of striking workers. They need computers and printers to publish pamphlets and exchange e-mail. They need Western govern-

---

* www.memri.org/bin/opener_latest.cgi?ID=SD54803.

ments and human rights groups to know their names and care about their fates, so that the Iranian government understands that it will be held responsible if they vanish.

Above all, Iran's dissidents need the consistent and vocal support of the United States. They need us to make clear that we regard Iran's current government as illegitimate and intolerable and that we support the brave souls who are struggling to topple it.

The United States has done almost none of those things. Why do we hesitate?

The foreign policy bureaucracy offers two arguments in favor of a passive approach to the Iranian crisis. First, it contends that the United States is legally obliged to refrain from attempting to undermine the Iranian government by the terms of the 1981 deal that freed the fifty-two American hostages Iran seized and held for 444 days. This rationale cannot be serious. Even if the United States made such a concession at the time, it was extracted under duress and can hardly be regarded as binding. The second argument the bureaucracy offers is that our support for the Iranian freedom movement will only further embitter the Iranian government against us. But the mullahs are plenty bitter as it is. They are determined to destroy us, and they will do their utmost to achieve that end whatever we do. In their paranoia, they will believe that we are aiding their dissidents whether we actually do so or not.

These flimsy objections do not really explain the bureaucracy's animus to the Iranian freedom movement. The same

State Department that now disdains Iranian exiles previously disdained Iraqi and Russian exiles. If it tries to persuade President Bush not to support Iranian dissidents today, it is for the same reason that it not so long ago tried to dissuade President Reagan from supporting the freedom movement in the Eastern bloc.

At bottom, at absolute rock bottom, our diplomats begin all their work with a fundamental institutional prejudice. It is their business to deal with foreign governments. The question "*Should* we be dealing with this government?" is simply alien to their whole professional outlook. Except in very rare cases (apartheid South Africa, for example), our diplomats cannot help regarding all the world's governments, no matter how objectionable, as essentially *legitimate*. Nor can they help mistrusting all U.S. attempts to overturn a government, no matter how eagerly that government's people would welcome liberation, as essentially illegitimate. When pressed by a bold president like Reagan, they may grudgingly acknowledge that the peoples of the world are theoretically entitled to live in freedom. But they will then argue that American action to help those peoples gain their freedom will always be too risky and the consequences too unpredictable, just as they once argued that it would be too risky and unpredictable to support the liberation of central and Eastern Europe.

We sense that the American people take a very different view. The American people do not yearn to charge about the world overturning governments. They understand that American power has its limits and that often the United States will reluctantly have to do business with foreign leaders Americans dislike or even despise. But we suspect that they feel, as we do, that the legitimacy and authority of undemocratic governments are inherently suspect. A Robert Mugabe, a Fidel Castro, and, yes, an Ayatollah Ali Khamenei have no more right to control Zimbabwe, Cuba, or Iran than any other criminal has to seize control of the persons and property of others. It's not always in our power to do anything about such criminals, nor is it always in our interest, but when it is in our power and our interest, we should toss dictators aside with no more compunction than a police sharpshooter feels when he downs a hostage-taker. We cannot create democracy at will. But we are not obliged to honor the pretensions of nondemocratic governments, either.

Those in our government who oppose aiding Iran's dissidents offer this one final point: They note that the dissidents may very well fail. This point is obviously valid. Failure is always a possibility, except when we refuse to try—then it is a certainty.

Syria

IF ALL OUR problems were as easy as Syria, the war on terror would have ended a year ago. Here is a regime that is surrounded by U.S. and allied forces; that depends for fuel on oil exports from Iraq; and whose economy is a pitiful shambles. Really, there is only one question to ask about Syria: Why have we put up with it as long as we have?

Our policy toward Syria should be stern and uncompromising. We should interdict the movement of weapons from Iran to Syria by air and sea. We should halt the flow of oil to Syria from Iraq. We should avail ourselves of the right of hot pursuit to follow suspected terrorists from Iraq into Syria. On the other hand, we should offer to provide Syria with generous economic aid in return for a Westward reorientation of its policy:

1. Syria must cease all support for terrorists, close all terrorist offices on its territory, stop providing sanctuary and support for Hezbollah, and surrender any terrorists on its territory or in Lebanon who are implicated in crimes against Americans, including the 1983 marine barracks bombing.

2. It must close its border to Iraqi guerrillas and surrender any and all Baathist leaders who have fled into Syria.

3. We expect Syria to cease its campaign of incitement against Israel, which only nourishes the culture of suicide bombing.

4. Syria must withdraw its forces from Lebanon and recognize that country's independence and sovereignty. If the Lebanese need help patrolling and policing their territory, we can arrange for them to get it from a less domineering source.

5. Finally: Syria must open its controlled economy and its authoritarian political system. For more than three decades, the Assad family has ruled Syria as a terrorist-

sponsoring private collection agency, and they have been rewarded with attention and flattery from every U.S. president since Richard Nixon. Secretary of State Warren Christopher alone paid twenty-nine visits to Syria, more than he paid to any member of the NATO alliance. It may offend every instinct of the accommodationists in our foreign policy bureaucracy, but it is past time to see whether the talented nation of Syria cannot produce leaders who have something to offer besides tyranny and war.

We doubt that Bashir Assad will welcome these requests. Under the circumstances, though, it should not be impossible to convince him that the consequences of refusing them will be considerably graver for him than the consequences of acquiescing.

Libya

LIBYA HAS A long history of support for terrorism that is in no way expunged by its promise to pay compensation to the families of the victims of the Lockerbie atrocity. The promise to pay has been extracted by intense pressure, which, were that the end of the story, would be perfectly all right. But the Libyans have demanded concessions from us as part of the bargain, and that is not all right. The Bush administration has rightly rebuffed Libya's demand to be removed from the list of terror-sponsoring states. If Libya wants off the list, all it need do is sever its associations with terrorist organizations.

Its denials notwithstanding, Libya is aggressively pursuing weapons of mass destruction of all sorts, chemical, biological, and nuclear. Libya should be regarded and treated as what it is: an implacably hostile regime. The illusion that Muammar al-Qaddafi is "moderating" should be treated as what *it* is: a symptom of the seemingly incurable wishful delusions that afflict the accommodationists in the foreign policy establishment.

The Dark Places

"AND THIS ALSO has been one of the dark places of the earth." So observes Marlow in Joseph Conrad's *Heart of Darkness* as he surveys the crowded shipyards of the Thames. And it is in today's dark places, beyond the reach of law, that terrorists now skulk and hide. These dark places are sometimes referred to as "failed states," but this term is too precise. There are indeed places where terrorists have gained a foothold because political authority has collapsed—places like Somalia or Sierra Leone or the jungles of Colombia. But Taliban Afghanistan was not a failed state. Indeed, the Taliban gave Afghanistan its strongest government in decades, even centuries. Lebanon, Hezbollah's home base, is not a failed state, either, at least not from the point of view of its masters in Damascus. For them, Lebanon is a highly *successful* state that functions exactly as they would wish it to—as a place from which they can deal drugs, wage war on Israel, and do dirty business, all while disclaiming any responsibility for their own actions. If al-Qaeda is beginning to make itself at home in some remoter areas of Venezuela, it is because the government of General Hugo Chávez has invited it in. In Paraguay and Brazil, Hezbollah has gained its foothold because a corrupt government has opted to look the other way. If it ever stopped paying off the local authorities, it would discover that South American governments can be more than effective when they choose.

Terrorists find sanctuary for almost as many different reasons as there are sanctuaries for them to find. Sometimes a government simply is unable to root them out of a remote or inaccessible portion of its national territory—as the Filipino government has tried and failed to root out the Abu Sayyaf guerrillas of Mindanao island or as the Indonesians have tried and failed in Aceh.

At the other extreme, governments collude with the terrorists on their soil, as the Taliban did, as the Sudanese have done, as Iraq did, as Syria and Iran now do, as the Palestinian Authority (PA) exists to do, and as General Chávez seems tempted to do.

In other cases, we may find that a government could take action against terrorists but for reasons of fear or corruption chooses not to act, as in Paraguay, and as may now be happening in northern Nigeria.

Finally, there are places where law truly has collapsed and evil has moved in to exploit the void: Yemen, Somalia, Sierra Leone.

Each of these situations calls for a different kind of response.

Where a government is struggling against terrorists within its boundaries, we must offer all the help in our power—not least to the government of Great Britain, which can with considerable justice complain that in the past the United States has turned a blind eye to fund-raising on our soil by the Irish Republican Army. We should be intensifying our cooperation with the Indonesians, whose civilian government has belatedly awakened to the gravity of the threat from Islamic extremism.

On the other hand, those governments that collude with terror should feel the full rigor of President Bush's rule that you are either with us or you are with the terrorists.

But in the intermediate cases—where a government acquiesces in terrorism because it is too weak to act against it, or where government has collapsed altogether and cannot exert authority—we should take our guidance from a president who lived one hundred years ago: Theodore Roosevelt. In his annual message to Congress in December 1904, he enunciated a policy that has since become known as the Roosevelt Corollary to the Monroe Doctrine. If possible, it possesses more relevance today than it did on the day Roosevelt propounded it:

> If a nation shows that it knows how to act with reasonable efficiency and decency in social and political matters, if it keeps order and pays its obligations, it need fear no interference from the United States. Chronic wrongdoing, or an impotence which results in a general loosening of the ties of civilized society, may in America,

as elsewhere, ultimately require intervention by some civilized nation, and in the Western Hemisphere the adherence of the United States to the Monroe Doctrine may force the United States, however reluctantly, in flagrant cases of such wrongdoing or impotence, to the exercise of an international police power.*

National sovereignty is an obligation as well as an entitlement. A government that will not perform the role of a government forfeits the rights of a government. The United States has acted on this principle since its founding. The Barbary States that raided American shipping during the Jefferson administration were theoretically provinces of the Ottoman Empire. The Ottomans could not stop their piracy—so we sent Commodore Decatur to do the job instead. When civil order collapsed in Mexico after the revolution of 1910, and bandits raided American towns from across the border, the high-minded President Wilson ordered General Pershing to track down the bandits and kill them.

The United Nations system was founded upon the fiction of the equal competence of all the world's governments, of which there are now more than 160. A vast international bureaucracy sustains and enforces the pretense that Cameroon is a state in the same sense that Canada is, that Nepal is functionally equivalent to the Netherlands. The clear-eyed wisdom of the Roosevelt Corollary—which recognized that if the United States didn't keep order in the Caribbean, the Ger-

---

* Annual message to Congress, December 6, 1904.

mans or British would—gave way to the idealistic hopes of the UN Charter that we could all keep order *together*.

Those hopes crumbled to dust a long, long time ago. And now, a century later, an updated version of the Roosevelt Corollary seems to be reemerging as the international law of nations. When Sierra Leone collapsed, Britain stepped in to keep order. The United States did the same in Liberia. German and Canadian troops patrol Afghanistan, the French police Bosnia, and the Australians lend a hand in East Timor. And surely this is right. When drought or famine lays waste to a poor country, the world's wealthy countries band together to send food and relief. How are we justified in turning our backs when the country is ravaged by human wrongdoers rather than by natural disaster? And when these wrongdoers threaten us—or create opportunities for terrorists who intend to threaten us—then the moral case for intervention is reinforced by the unignorable dictates of self-interest.

Hamas and Hezbollah

HAMAS AND HEZBOLLAH (and Yasser Arafat's Al-Aqsa Brigades as well) are often the beneficiaries of special exemptions from the usual condemnation of terrorism. "You can't say that the whole of Hamas is a terrorist organization and certainly that is not our position": So declared the European Union's spokesman on June 29, 2003, as he announced that the EU would continue to take no action against the so-called political wing of Hamas. Under intense pressure from the Bush administration, the EU reversed itself in September 2003. But the impulse to condone Hamas and Hezbollah is deeply embedded.

During the 2002 summit of French-speaking world leaders in Beirut, Madame Chirac took time to tour a Hamas-run refugee camp in Lebanon. Canada's foreign minister Bill Graham has waged a desperate battle to allow Hezbollah to continue to raise funds and do business in his country: "It is important not to label [elected officials], doctors, and teachers as terrorists," he said in November 2002—before outraged public opinion forced his colleagues to overrule him. The European Union has named individual Hezbollah leaders as terrorists, but not the group as a whole—it remains, for now, free to do its evil work on the European continent.

Hamas and Hezbollah do not run social welfare organizations out of the goodness of their hearts. They run them to win support from civilian populations that might otherwise fear and resent them. Terrorism is bad for the economy. Under Israeli occupation, the West Bank and Gaza in 1967–1987 posted some of the highest growth rates in the Arab world; since the outbreak of the Oslo war in September 2000, per capita incomes in the Palestinian territories have by most estimates dropped some 90 percent. And terrorism is also dangerous for the populations among whom the terrorists base themselves. Terrorists provoke retaliations in which civilians are bound to suffer. Palestinian terrorists—aware of the unusual global interest in their cause—have specialized in maximizing the exposure of civilians to Israeli retaliation. And when the Israelis have refused to retaliate brutally enough for the terrorists' purposes, the terrorists do the retaliating themselves, as they did in the world-famous case of Mohammed al-Dura, the twelve-year-old boy killed in his father's arms, supposedly in the crossfire of an Israeli-Palestinian gun battle in September 2000. Exhaustive ballistics research and careful scrutiny of the video evidence confirms beyond reasonable doubt that the footage that purports to document al-Dura's death was certainly staged—and that if al-Dura was killed at all, he was killed by Palestinian gunmen, very possibly deliberately.*

The soup kitchens and clinics run by Hamas and Hezbollah build the terrorist groups' prestige, help them recruit new killers, and give them plausible cover stories for their fundraising abroad. Of course, the donors must suspect—and the EU commissioners and the Canadian government well know—how absurd these cover stories are. People who make excuses for Hamas and Hezbollah are asking us to believe that organizations that do not hesitate to blow up buses of schoolchildren would never, ever dream of siphoning money from their welfare funds into their funds for murder.

The officials of Canada and the EU are too intelligent to believe such fables. They have quite another reason for their soft line on Hamas and Hezbollah: They seem to have

---

* See the review of the case by James Fallows: "Who Shot Mohammed al-Dura?," *Atlantic Monthly,* June 2003, available at www.theatlantic.com/issues/2003/06/fallows.htm.

adopted a scale of terrorist activity with different gradations of unacceptability. For them, terrorist attacks on Israel should not be compared to terrorist attacks in Paris or Toronto. Nor is it only foreign governments that condemn some terrorists more forcefully than others. The U.S. State Department again and again sends its spokesman Richard Boucher out before the cameras of the world to draw distinctions between terror groups that murder Israelis and terror groups that attack Americans. Actually, Boucher does not so much draw the distinctions as simply insist on them. Within the space of two weeks in September 2002, for example, Boucher was called on first to condemn an Israeli-targeted attack on a Hamas terrorist leader in the West Bank and then to defend an American-targeted attack on an al-Qaeda leader in Yemen. When queried on this seeming contradiction, he asserted that the justifications for American-targeted killings "do not necessarily apply in other circumstances." Why not? "We all understand . . . the situation with regard to Israeli-Palestinian issues and the prospects of peace and the prospects of negotiation and the prospects of the need to create an atmosphere for progress." It's a very strange idea of "progress" that would grant immunity to one of the world's deadliest terrorist movements.

The distinction between Islamic terrorism against Israel, on the one hand, and Islamic terrorism against the United States and Europe, on the other, cannot be sustained.

Hamas and al-Qaeda seem to raise their money from the same sources and are quietly assisted by many of the same influential people in Saudi Arabia. Hezbollah's South American infrastructure offers concealment to al-Qaeda operatives in this hemisphere. Likewise, European reluctance to act against European supporters of Hamas and Hezbollah protects European supporters of al-Qaeda as well.

Worse, the ideology that justifies the terrible crimes of Hamas and Hezbollah is the same ideology that justifies the crimes of al-Qaeda. If it's okay to blow up civilians in a holy war against Israel, it is equally okay to blow them up in a holy war against India, or Russia, or us. We would not have got very far against Nazism if we had said, "It's wrong to shove Poles, gypsies, and the mentally impaired into gas chambers, but it's perfectly fine to do it to the Jews." Likewise, we won't get very far against the ideology of global jihad as long as we suggest that some terrorist jihads are acceptable forms of "resistance" while others are not.

The Islamic world understands this even if the French or the Canadians or the State Department do not. Consider the case of Sheikh Yousuf al-Qaradawi, dean of Islamic studies at the University of Qatar and one of the most respected of Sunni Muslim clerics. In 2001, al-Qaradawi condemned the 9/11 attacks (assuming, he said, that "such attacks were carried out by a Muslim, as some biased groups claim").* Al-Qaradawi has consistently supported Hamas's suicide attacks in Israel—and his reasons, explained at some length at a conference in Stockholm in July 2003, should give pause to those

* www.islamonline.net/English/News/2001-09/13/article25.shtml.

who believe that the jihad ideology can be contained inside the West Bank.

"It has been determined by Islamic law that the blood and property of people of *Dar al-Harb* [the Domain of Disbelief—that is, the non-Muslim world] is not protected. Because they fight against and are hostile towards the Muslims, they annulled the protection of his blood and his property."

Nor is the distinction between civilians and noncivilians relevant to jihad. "In modern war, all of society, with all its classes and ethnic groups, is mobilized to participate in the war, to aid its continuation, and to provide it with the material and human fuel required for it to assure the victory of the state fighting its enemies. Every citizen in society must take upon himself a role in the effort to provide for the battle. The entire domestic front, including professionals, laborers, and industrialists, stands behind the fighting army, even if it does not bear arms."

Finally, according to al-Qaradawi, suicide bombers should not be considered to violate Islam's injunctions against self-inflicted death. "While the [person who commits] suicide dies in escape and retreat, the one who carries out a martyrdom operation dies in advance and attack. Unlike the [person who commits] suicide, who has no goal except escape from confrontation, the one who carries out a martyrdom operation has a clear goal, and that is to please Allah. . . ."*

Al-Qaradawi may wish to limit the applicability of these

---

* www.memri.org/bin/articles.cgi?Page=subjects&Area=jihad&ID=SP54203.

principles to Jews and Indians. But there is no shortage of people ready to seize those words and broaden them to include all infidels. Agence France-Presse reported in February 2002 that Hamas was circulating leaflets in the West Bank designating the United States as an enemy equal to Israel: "America, in supporting the Zionists and ignoring the rights of Palestinians, carries responsibility for the crimes of the occupying forces."[*] Sheikh Ahmad Yassin, the leader of Hamas, refers whenever he thinks the media are not listening to the "American-Zionist enemy."[†] Al-Qaradawi himself, in his fiery moods, has hinted that America is an appropriate target for jihad: When Baghdad was liberated, he described President Bush as the "new Hulago"—Hulago being the Mongol khan who captured Baghdad in 1258, overthrew the caliphate, and has been blamed by Arab historians for all the woes the Arab world has suffered in the following 750 years. Al-Qaradawi calls the United States "the invader" and "the enemy," demands the release from prison of Sheikh Omar Abdel Rahman (the instigator of the 1993 World Trade Center bombing), and criticized the May 12, 2003, terror attacks in Riyadh because "not everyone who was killed in Riyadh was American. . . ."[‡]

Until Muslim opinion accepts that suicide bombings that

---

[*] "Hamas Accuses United States of Declaring War on Muslims and Arabs," Agence France-Presse, February 1, 2002.

[†] See, for example, this exchange, dated May 7, 2003, on the Islam Online Web site: www.islamonline.net/livedialogue/english/Browse.asp?hGuestID=XbQ5ap.

[‡] www.memri.org/bin/articles.cgi?Page=subjects&Area=jihad&ID=SP53103.

target civilians are war crimes and that suicide bombers are war criminals—until suicide bombers are perceived as shaming Islam rather than glorifying it—the suicide bombings will continue. Those who encourage the Arab and Muslim world in the idea that *some* jihad murders are permissible are tacitly aiding those who argue that *all* jihad murders are permissible.

We cannot always compel other nations to act against all terror groups. But we can do this:

1. Purge from our own institutional thinking the illusory distinction between the "political" and "military" wings of terrorist organizations. These distinctions are a fraud.

2. Cease criticizing Israel for taking actions against Hamas and Hezbollah analogous to those the United States is taking against al-Qaeda.

3. Focus public attention on those of our allies who permit Hamas and Hezbollah or similar groups to operate on their territory. There's a term for this kind of complaisance: "harboring terrorism." If France does it, the United States should not scruple to say so.

4. As long as Hamas and other terrorist groups operate uncontrolled inside the Palestinian Authority—and as long as Hezbollah is permitted to occupy most of southern Lebanon—then the PA and Lebanon's effective ruler, Syria, should be deemed state sponsors of terrorism and thus vulnerable to all the sanctions that U.S. law and policy mete out to those implicated in murder as an act of policy.

Saudi Arabia

THE RULERS OF Saudi Arabia claim to be staunch friends of the United States in the war on terror. Their behavior suggests otherwise.

In January 2001, two of the future 9/11 hijackers flew into San Diego to begin preparations for their attack. At the airport, they were met by a Saudi man, Omar al-Bayoumi, an employee of the Saudi civil aviation authority and a man known for his keen interest in the doings of Saudi citizens in the San Diego area. Al-Bayoumi drove the two future hijackers into town and arranged for them to rent an apartment next to his. He guaranteed the lease for them, too, and plunked down $1,550 in cash to cover the first two months' rent. Then he threw them a welcoming party. Later, he helped the men open bank accounts, obtain Social Security cards—and enroll in flight school. Oh, one more detail: While al-Bayoumi was aiding the two terrorists, he was receiving through his wife tens of thousands of dollars in gifts from the wife of the Saudi ambassador to the United States. Those payments increased after he hosted the two future hijackers.

Al-Bayoumi left the United States in July 2001. He is now living in Saudi Arabia. It took nearly two years of diplomatic pressure—culminating in a direct personal request from Condoleezza Rice to Saudi foreign minister Prince Saud—to persuade the Saudis to permit al-Bayoumi to be questioned by U.S. investigators. Al-Bayoumi has denied all advance knowledge of the 9/11 terror attacks.

The case of Omar al-Bayoumi is only one of the many mysterious connections between the Saudi ruling elite and al-Qaeda. The $1 trillion lawsuit filed against the Saudi government by families of the 9/11 victims alleges that Prince Turki Faisal, then the kingdom's intelligence chief, met twice with representatives of al-Qaeda and offered them large sums of money to spare Saudi targets. The lawsuit also alleges that the prince's own accountant distributed more than $1 million to al-Qaeda cells in Europe, including Mohammed Atta's Hamburg cell.* Prince Turki has vehemently denied these accusations.

As recently as November 2002, the Saudi embassy in Washington aided a Saudi woman under federal subpoena to flee the country.

Saudi Arabia is the single largest source of money and men for al-Qaeda and for other terrorist groups as well. According to the most scrupulous account we have, al-Qaeda has collected between $300 million and $500 million in donations since the late 1980s, almost all of it from sources inside Saudi Arabia.† Seven individuals whose identities are known to the United States have been unusually consistent and generous donors. There is considerable overlap between the al-Qaeda donors in Saudi Arabia and the wealthy individuals and members of the royal family who provide more than half of the annual budget of Hamas and significant sums

---

* observer.guardian.co.uk/international/story/0,6903,905698,00.html.

† Jean-Charles Brisard, "Terrorism Financing: Roots and Trends of Saudi Terrorism Financing," Report to the UN Security Council, December 19, 2002.

too to Islamic Jihad, as well as hundreds of thousands of dollars to the families of Palestinian suicide bombers.*

Poorer Saudi Arabians give their lives instead of their money to the terror cause. In an August 2003 interview on the Arabic-language television station al-Jazeera, Deputy Secretary of State Richard Armitage, never a man needlessly to affront Saudi sensibilities, ranked Saudi Arabia alongside Iran and Syria as the point of origin of the foreign terrorists infiltrating into Iraq.† Armitage declined to say whether the governments of any of these three countries were implicated in the infiltration. But the Saudi government's record of support for terror-tainted Islamic organizations is indisputable. Dore Gold, an Israeli expert on Saudi Arabia, reports that after September 11, a raid on the Sarajevo offices of the Saudi High Commission for Aid to Bosnia found computer programs to simulate the best way for crop-duster aircraft to spread chemical weapons, along with maps of Washington, D.C., that had government buildings marked with bull's-eyes.‡ The Saudi government gives millions of dollars a year to the Al-Haramain Islamic Foundation; in March 2002, the U.S. Treasury placed Al-Haramain on the list of institutions that have

---

* Hamas's annual budget is variously estimated at anywhere from $12 million to $30 million. In March 2002, Israeli forces in the city of Tulkarm in the West Bank discovered an itemized list of 102 families who had received a total of $545,000 from the Saudi government's Saudi Committee for Aid to the Al-Quds Intifada. In April 2002, Saudi state television staged a telethon that raised more than $100 million in pledges to support the Palestinian terror war.

† asia.reuters.com/newsArticle.jhtml?type=topNews&storyID=3324095.

‡ Dore Gold, *Hatred's Kingdom: How Saudi Arabia Supports the New Global Terrorism* (Regnery, 2003), p. 146.

provided aid to terrorism. By its own estimate, the Saudi government has contributed some $4 billion to the Palestinian Authority's campaign against Israel since 1998.*

The Saudi record of direct aid to terror is only the tip of the spear of a larger Saudi effort to spread its extremist version of Islam through the Muslim world and into Europe and North America. Since the 1970s, the Saudi government has spent many billions of dollars to support Islamic religious colleges in Pakistan and (as we have seen) Islamic day schools in the United States; to convert felons in British and American jails to Islam; to bulk up the incomes of Egyptian and other Arab clerics who teach extremist versions of Islam at the region's universities—and to support American academic institutions that soothe Americans with honeyed assurances that nothing is to be feared from extremist Islam. Again by Saudi estimates, their money has built in the non-Muslim world some 210 Islamic centers, more than 1,500 mosques, and almost 2,000 Islamic schools. In these institutions, moderate and tolerant interpretations of Islam are excluded in favor of the Saudis' own extreme creed. In the Muslim world, Saudi money has wrought even greater harm. From Java to Nigeria, Saudi funds have smothered broad-minded indigenous Muslim traditions and paid instead for schools, mosques, and teachers who glorify jihad and teach hatred—not only of the West, but also of Muslim governments that in any way fall short of the most extreme interpretations of the requirements

* www.memri.org/bin/articles.cgi?Page=countries&Area=saudiarabia&ID=SR1703.

of the faith. And through it all, Saudi Arabia's own preachers, religious instructors, and journalists preach hate-filled sermons, teach the most frightful lies, and disseminate the deadliest conspiracy theories. Twice in recent months, Saudi government newspapers have published articles repeating the terrible old charge of Jewish ritual murder, one of them by a professor at King Faisal University.*

Why do the Saudis do it? After all, the Saudi ruling class is not exactly famous for its desert austerity and Muslim rectitude. Even the regime's designated American apologist, Saudi ambassador Prince Bandar bin Sultan, is willing to acknowledge that the Saudi elite has stolen or misappropriated something like $50 billion of the country's oil wealth over the past thirty years.†

The Australian American reporter Geraldine Brooks tells this story about an interview with a member of the Saudi ruling elite in the fall of 1990:

> His glass-walled study looked out on a floodlit swimming pool and a flower-filled courtyard. If the wall were not glass, he explained, he wouldn't be able to sit with me. "If a man and a woman are alone together, the third person present is Satan," he said. After about an hour I closed my notebook and thanked him for the interview. Showing me to the door, he paused, as an afterthought, and asked if I'd like to meet a few of his friends. Of course, I said.

* memri.org/bin/articles.cgi?Page=archives&Area=sd&ID=SP35402.
† www.pbs.org/wgbh/pages/frontline/shows/terrorism/interviews/bandar.html.

Stepping across the hall, he opened a door on a dimly lit room full of blaring rock music and entangled bodies. A gorgeous Filipina in a black Spandex mini-dress was dancing, rubbing herself rhythmically against her white-robed partner. Another man sat cross-legged on the floor, flashing a colored light at her legs. On sunken couches, a beautiful blond-maned Turk[ish woman] caressed an Egyptian woman for the benefit of a smiling male voyeur. At a bar in the corner, guests helped themselves to Johnnie Walker whiskey—$135 a bottle on the black market and its consumption punishable by flogging in the city square. . . .

When I rose to leave, the Filipina asked if she could get a lift with my driver. She reached for her abaya—the Arabian version of the chador—and face veil. Aware of the men's eyes on her, she twitched the black silk slowly forward, letting it insinuate itself inch by inch over her cleavage and pour slowly down her thighs. Taking the piece of gauze that covers the face, she tossed her long tresses forward, leaning suggestively toward the men for a moment, then turning slightly to provide a view of her curvaceous rump. She flipped her head back, catching all her hair in the veil. It was a reverse strip tease. At the end of it she stood there, a black cone, the picture of Saudi female probity.*

But really, there is no contradiction to explain. It is precisely the corruption of the Saudi ruling class that impels many of its members to support extremist Islam. From its origins 250 years ago, the Saudi royal family—and the hangers-

* Geraldine Brooks, *Nine Parts of Desire: The Hidden World of Islamic Women* (Anchor Books, 1996), pp. 47–48.

on whom they have enriched—have rested their claim to rule on their zeal for the most militant version of the Islamic faith. The price they pay for the right to carouse with luscious women in private is their stern enforcement of the *abaya* in public.

For three decades, the United States has underwritten and tacitly endorsed this Saudi-Wahhabi deal. We decided in the 1970s that the Saudi monarchy was a safe and sound custodian of the oil fields of the Gulf, so we acquiesced in everything the Saudi princes claimed they needed to do in order to stay in power, no matter how humiliating to the United States. When President Bush visited the troops in Saudi Arabia at Thanksgiving 1990, he was told that no Christian worship, not even grace before the meal, would be permitted on Saudi soil. The president ate his turkey aboard a U.S. warship.

But as the Saudi regime has faltered economically and as the regime's corruption has become notorious, the Saudi-Wahhabi relationship has begun to disintegrate. Over the past decade, the regime has been hit again and again by Islamic terror attacks. In November 1995, a truck bomb killed five Americans and two Indian nationals at a Saudi National Guard training center. In June 1996, the Khobar Towers attack killed nineteen Americans. Three car bombings in November 2000 killed one Briton and seriously wounded five other foreign nationals.

Through it all, the kingdom's leaders reacted consistently: They did not want to know the truth. They executed the suspects in the National Guard truck bombing before they could be questioned by U.S. intelligence. The Saudis stonewalled the American investigation of the Khobar Towers. They responded to the Riyadh car bombings by blaming "bootleggers" and arresting five Britons, a Canadian, and a Belgian. Under torture, the men confessed; two of them were sentenced to death. The car bombings continued uninterrupted. (The arrested men were pardoned and returned home in August 2003.)

Even after 9/11, the denial continued. The Saudis refused to take action when presented with evidence that their citizens funded terror. They refused to allow American investigators to question Saudis on Saudi soil. They refused the United States access to Saudi financial records. They refused to act even when presented with formal allegations of Saudi nationals' involvement in terrorist financing. In August 2003, the Saudis presented us—as if it were a huge concession—with the news that a Saudi bank had closed the account of the most conspicuous of the suspected terrorist financiers. (Who says Saudi law is always draconian? A Saudi princess caught committing adultery will be stoned or beheaded. Filipino laborers caught attending Christian worship are jailed and tortured. But a man who is thought to have paid for mass murder has his checking privileges withdrawn.)

After the terrorist attacks of May 12, 2003, the Saudis vowed to cooperate with the United States in earnest. William Wechsler, who served on the NSC's counterterrorism team in the Clinton administration, aptly said of this latest

Saudi promise to be good: "What the Saudis have accomplished recently has been enough to prevent people from saying that they've done nothing or even next to nothing. They've done something now, and it's a good something that they've done. But 100 more of these little steps and they'll be at the minimum level of what they should be."* Will the Saudis take those steps? The U.S. government publicly lauds the cooperation it receives from the Saudis. In all probability, however, "the government will continue the same as before," concludes another analyst, anonymously. "That is, walking the tightrope between going after the trigger men while playing cozy with the infrastructure that feeds the extremists."† The Saudi rulers walk that tightrope for two reasons: Many of them fear their extremists more than they fear the United States. And the rest of them *are* the extremists whom the others fear. The Saudis have gotten away with walking the tightrope because we let them, because we have convinced ourselves that we have a bigger stake in the survival of the Saudi monarchy than the Saudis themselves.

What we should want from the Saudis is obvious and really unarguable: We want them to crack down on terrorist fund-raising within their borders. We want their government media to stop inciting terror. We want them to cooperate fully in the suppression of terror. And we want them to stop propagating jihad to the rest of the Islamic world and to

---

* Steven R. Weisman with Douglas Jehl, "Ambassador Says Saudis Didn't Heed Security Requests," *The New York Times,* May 15, 2003, p. A1.
† Ibid.

Muslim populations in the West. In short, we want them to act like the friend they say they are and not the disguised enemy their record suggests them to have been. If the Saudis were to do all that, they would continue to offend American values, but they would no longer menace American interests. If not . . . well then, it's hard to explain why we should care whether they survive. For thirty years, U.S. Saudi policy has been guided by the dogma that, problematic as the Saudi monarchy is, it is better than any likely alternative. September 11 should have dispelled that illusion forever. Yes, it's possible to imagine worse alternatives in the Arabian peninsula. Certainly the existing alternative is bad enough. But it is also possible to imagine better alternatives.

To improve that existing alternative, we should

1. Tell the truth about Saudi Arabia. It's past time to drop the happy talk about how splendidly the Saudis are cooperating. ("The Saudis have done everything we've asked them to.") These transparent untruths demean the U.S. government—worse, they encourage the Saudis in their arrogant belief that they can stiff the United States and get away with it. The Saudis qualify for their own membership in the axis of evil: They paid for some three-quarters of the cost of developing Pakistan's nuclear bomb—and without the Pakistani bomb, neither the Iranian nor the North Korean bomb would be as advanced as it is. The Saudis support terror on a lavish scale: A Saudi crackdown on terror financing would put al-Qaeda, Hamas, and Islamic Jihad

out of business. The Saudis shelter absconded persons of interest to the United States like Omar al-Bayoumi. The president of the United States should publicly acknowledge these realities—and demand that they change.

2. Punish those individual Saudis who finance terror. The Treasury Department should create a list of foreign individuals suspected of terrorist financing to match its list of suspect charities. Those individuals and their family members should be denied permission to set foot on American soil. It should be made a crime for Americans to do business with them or to do business with any third party who does business with them. If the Drug Enforcement Agency finds cocaine in the trunk of a car, it can impound the car and require the owner to prove that he was innocent of drug trafficking before he gets his vehicle back. In the same way, Treasury should be permitted to seize any U.S. assets belonging to a foreign terrorist financier—just as Treasury seized the property of those who traded with the enemy in 1917 and 1941.

3. Demand that the Saudis cease their Wahhabi missionary efforts in the United States and elsewhere abroad. It is intolerable that the Saudis should support imams who preach jihad to American ex-cons while the Americans who guard Saudi Arabia's borders are not permitted so much as a quiet Bible reading in the privacy of their barracks. We cannot compel the Saudis to stop what they do. But neither can we remain indifferent to what they do. President Bush has spoken eloquently about the suppres-

sion of religious liberty in Sudan and China. He should add mention of Saudi Arabia to the list: "There is now a mosque in Rome so that Muslims in the homeland of the Roman Catholic Church may freely practice their faith. Many millions of Roman Catholics from the Philippines and other countries live in Saudi Arabia. Yet they are not allowed to go to church or even to own a rosary. If they are caught worshipping with friends, they are liable to be arrested, tortured, and then deported. Modern Muslims should have the vision to live by the tolerant words of the Prophet: 'To you your religion; to me, my religion.' "

4. Warn the Saudis that anything less than their utmost cooperation in the war on terror will have the severest consequences for the Saudi state. A seldom noted fact about Saudi Arabia is that while the royal family, the government, and the moneyed elite all live on the western, Red Sea side of the country, the oil is located on the eastern, Persian Gulf side. And while the people of the west are almost uniformly Sunni, one-third of the people of the Eastern Province—to whom the oil might well have belonged had the fortunes of battle turned out a little differently in the 1920s—are Shiites. The State Department's most recent biennial human rights report notes "institutionalized discrimination against adherents of the minority Shi'a branch of Islam." The construction of Shiite mosques is not permitted, and the testimony of Shiites is often disregarded in court. Shiite children are required to attend Sunni schools. Shiite leaders have been arbitrarily arrested, tortured, and on occasion murdered. It is not big-

otry alone that explains these Saudi actions, but also their fear that the Shiites might someday seek independence for the Eastern Province—and its oil. Independence for the Eastern Province would obviously be a catastrophic outcome for the Saudi state. But it might be a very good outcome for the United States. Certainly it's an outcome to ponder. Even more certainly, we would want the Saudis to know that we are pondering it. The knowledge that the United States has options other than abjectly accepting whatever abuse the Saudis choose to throw our way might have a . . . chastening . . . effect on Saudi behavior.

There is one more thing that must be said, and it is a hard thing to say. The reason our policy toward Saudi Arabia has been so abject for so long is not mere error. Our policy has been abject because so many of those who make the policy have been bought and paid for by the Saudis—or else are looking forward to the day when they *will* be bought and paid for. The Saudi ambassador to the United States, Prince Bandar, "has told associates that he makes a point of staying close to officials who have worked with Saudi Arabia after they leave government service. 'If the reputation then builds that the Saudis take care of friends when they leave office,' Bandar once observed, according to a knowledgeable source, 'you'd be surprised how much better friends you have who are just coming into office.' "* With

* Robert G. Kaiser and David Ottaway, "Oil for Security Fueled Close Ties; But Major Differences Led to Tensions," *The Washington Post,* February 11, 2002, p. A1.

honorable exceptions like Hume Horan, who served Ronald Reagan, too many of our recent ambassadors to Saudi Arabia have served as shills for Saudi Arabia the instant they returned home. Daniel Pipes has proposed that former ambassadors be banned for ten years after their departure from accepting any funds from public or private interests in the country to which they had been accredited. That seems too legalistic to us. We would not have a problem with a former ambassador to Mexico joining the board of a Mexican company two or three years later or a former ambassador to Britain taking a teaching post at Oxford. Saudi Arabia presents a unique problem: Unlike Mexico and unlike Britain, it has over a quarter century spent hundreds of millions of dollars to corrupt the American political system. One picturesque example: Within a month of Bill Clinton's winning the Democratic presidential nomination in 1992, the Riyadh Chamber of Commerce donated $3.5 million to the University of Arkansas to create a "King Fahd Center for Middle East and Islamic Studies." One month after Clinton's inauguration, the University of Ar-kansas got $20 million more from the Saudis. When journalists follow policy debates over tobacco or health care or any other domestic issue, they identify which people are expressing their conscientious beliefs and which are the paid lobbyists. The American public should expect equal information when the topic is national security—and they are especially entitled to it when the lobbyist is lobbying for an unfriendly power.

How to Pay for the War

PRESIDENT BUSH'S REQUEST in the fall of 2003 for $87 billion for reconstruction in Iraq and Afghanistan has convinced a lot of people who hated his tax cut to begin with that they really, really hated his tax cut. *The Washington Post's* Steve Mufson warned:

> the request, which could push the federal budget deficit to more than $500 billion during the next fiscal year, should make people stop and wonder whether President Bush's 2001 and 2002 tax cuts significantly compromised America's ability to respond vigorously to problems at home and abroad in the future.*

It sometimes seems as if many people in the media object to everything about the war on terror except for the higher taxes they insist are necessary to pay for the war.

If it turns out that the costs of victory in the war on terror require temporary tax increases, then temporary tax increases we must have. But that's not what this argument is about. The tax cuts that President Bush's political opponents are most eager to repeal are the tax cuts that go into effect in 2005, 2006, and later—tax cuts that have no relevance to the war today, but that cramp and constrain their spending ambitions for tomorrow.

---

* Steve Mufson, "Show U.S. the Money: There Are 87 Billion Reasons to Revisit Those Tax Cuts, Mr. President," *The Washington Post,* September 14, 2003, p. B1.

Terror has imposed significant costs on the U.S. economy. Companies and governments have to pay for tighter security. It takes longer to move people and goods than it did before 9/11—and delays cost money. Above all, terror increases uncertainty about the future, depressing the willingness of investors and entrepreneurs to take risks. Since the terrorist attacks, the U.S. economy has had to bear new and unexpected burdens. President Bush's tax cuts have helped lighten the load.

The U.S. government can afford to pay for the war on terror out of current revenues. The U.S. government spends some $2 trillion a year. President Bush's $87 billion request for reconstruction aid amounts to less than 5 percent of the total. The budget is in deficit not because of the war, but because of the 2001–2002 recession and the sharp rise in health care costs that has pushed up spending on Medicare and Medicaid. President Bush's first budget director, Mitch Daniels, often made the point that Franklin Roosevelt cut domestic spending by almost 25 percent between 1940 and 1942 to help finance World War II. Some of Roosevelt's favorite programs—like the Civilian Conservation Corps— were abolished altogether. The war on terror will not cost anywhere near as much as World War II. Domestic spending will not have to be cut to pay for the war, but spending will have to be constrained, as President Bush has proposed.

President Bush's critics accuse him of failing to impose sufficient "sacrifices" on the American people. They perceive that the cost of the war probably will preclude major new social programs. Some of those critics even paranoically allege that the war is a right-wing plot to forestall those social programs and win reelection in 2004.

But fighting wars is a very risky way to seek popularity. Korea did not help President Truman; Vietnam did not do much for Lyndon Johnson and Richard Nixon. President Bush did not seek this war on terror. He was as surprised by it as anybody, and it frightened his political advisers from the start. Many of them wanted him to wrap the war up immediately after the victory in Afghanistan and return to domestic issues in 2003 and 2004.

Bush is fighting the war on terror for the same reason that America is fighting the war on terror—because he and we have no choice. The enemy attacked us. However, we do not have to weaken the economy to pay for the war. We can pay for it by holding the line on federal spending, setting tax rates at levels that promote economic growth, and borrowing the remainder. We borrowed to win the Civil War, borrowed more to win World War I and World War II, borrowed again to win the cold war. Victory triggers economic prosperity—which in turn repays the debt we incurred to achieve the victory. How to pay for the war? The same steady answer that yields growth and prosperity in more normal times: keep taxes low, keep domestic spending under control, and borrow responsibly.

6. THE WAR OF IDEAS

THE WAR AGAINST extremist Islam is as much an ideological war as the cold war ever was. And despite all our successes on the battleground, the ideological struggle against extremist Islam is one we are losing—that is, when we bother to wage it at all.

In the first shock of 9/11, the Bush administration launched an ambitious campaign to woo the world's Muslims. The president went to mosques to stress his deep personal respect for the Muslim faith. Muslim dignitaries were welcomed to the White House to observe the Ramadan fast. A high-powered advertising executive was hired as undersecretary of state for public diplomacy to "rebrand" the United States in the eyes of Muslims worldwide. She backed the creation of a new Arabic-language radio station that broadcast pop tunes and terse, neutral news bulletins—and helped create a series of advertisements that showcased successful Muslim immigrants to the United States, including a New York Fire Department paramedic whose family had come from Kashmir and an Indonesian graduate student at school in Missouri.

This early public relations campaign was founded upon one crucial assumption: The most important reason extremism flourished in the Muslim world was that Muslims believed *we* were hostile to *them*. Some advocates of the Islamic outreach campaign went further still. They politely suggested that Islamic anti-Americanism, while unquestionably deplorable, should be regarded as an understandable reaction to the materialism and hedonism of American life, as refracted through MTV, pornography, and the Internet. At one point, it was even seriously considered that President Bush should mention in a speech that he was not always proud of the face America presented to the world.

After 9/11, the president did right, absolutely right, to warn Americans against indiscriminate anger and to remind them of the equal rights due to all Americans, regardless of origin or creed. We can all be proud of the extraordinary rarity of anti-Muslim hate crimes after 9/11—and President Bush deserves credit for his urgent admonitions against bigotry.

However, a nation that had exhibited the courage and self-sacrifice, the national unity and strength of purpose, that Americans showed in New York and Washington on 9/11 had no reason to apologize to anyone for its culture. And proceeding beyond calls for tolerance to the active propitiation of Muslim opinion at home and abroad was not merely undignified, but dangerous. Here's why:

One of the most powerful arguments that moderate Muslims deploy against terrorism is that it disgraces the good name of Muslims and Islam. The extremists claim, on the contrary, that spectacular acts of terrorism *strengthen* Islam. Listen to Osama bin Laden exulting over the effects of the 9/11 attacks in a videotape aired December 13, 2001: "In Holland, at one of the [Islamic] centers, the number of people who accepted Islam during the days that followed the operations were more than the people who accepted Islam in the last eleven years." Bin Laden said that he had "heard someone on Islamic radio who owns a school in America say, 'We don't have time to keep up with the demands of those who are asking about Islamic books to learn about Islam.' This event made people think [about Islam], which benefited Islam greatly."

The administration's solicitude for Muslim sensitivities might well have been interpreted by many Muslims as a vindication of bin Laden's methods. When before had an American president ever shown such deference to Islam? When had so many Western writers, journalists, and commentators listened so assiduously to the grievances and complaints of the Muslim world—and then repeated them so credulously to their audiences?

And to the administration's credit, it quickly recognized the folly of its initial approach. When President Bush visited a Washington-area school to encourage children to write to a pen pal in the Persian Gulf at the same time anthrax was showing up in the nation's mail slots, even the liberal press scoffed and protested. By then it was apparent that the courtship of organized Muslim opinion had emboldened the most extreme elements in the American Muslim community without winning the United States *any* new friends in the Islamic world.

The White House quietly backed away from an increasingly embarrassing dead end. After 9/11, a glamorous "Coalition Information Center" (CIC) was set up in grand quarters in the Indian Treaty Room in the Executive Office Building (EOB), complete with clocks giving the time in every war zone and the first flat-screen displays in the EOB. By the end of 2002, the CIC had quietly gone out of business; the high-powered advertising exec at Public Diplomacy resigned for health reasons in March 2003. Since then, Public Diplomacy has reverted to its accustomed (low) place in the bureaucratic scheme of things. At the end of July 2003, Deputy Defense Secretary Paul Wolfowitz complained in an interview on American television about al-Jazeera's incitement against U.S. forces in Iraq—incitement that was all the more effective because there was still no countervailing anti-Saddam, pro-Western voice on the Iraqi airwaves.*

No longer knowing what to say, we have fallen silent. But the silence of 2004 is as unseemly and dangerous as the cringing style of communication we practiced in 2001. If we do not tell our own story, others will tell it for us.

Yet this war of ideas is not primarily a war of words. Our words are not convincing, not only because the people of the Middle East do not believe what we say, but also because

---

* In large part because the Department of State had blocked plans by the Iraqi National Congress to establish an anti-Saddam broadcasting facility.

they and we do not agree on the meaning of the words that make up our moral vocabulary. Both Americans and Middle Easterners may agree, for example, that it is wrong to kill innocent human life. But we do not agree on who is and who is not "innocent." It is striking, for example, that for months after 9/11, American spokesmen continued to claim that the terrorist attackers had killed "hundreds" of Muslims, as Secretary of State Colin Powell said in a speech to the Agency for International Development as late as November 2, 2001. Powell must by then have had a pretty fair idea that this claim could not possibly be true. But Powell must also have understood that a terrorist attack whose victims were *not* Muslim was much less likely to trouble the consciences of the Islamic world.

It is a sad fact of human nature that we are much more sensitive to our own suffering than we are to the suffering of others. As long as Adolf Hitler killed only Jews, Poles, French, and Russians, he remained remarkably popular in Germany. It was only when the war he started brought British and American bombs tumbling down upon their own heads that the Germans began to curse his name.

In the same way, we must abandon the unrealistic idea that we will win over the Muslim Middle East by appealing to their sympathy for the grief and loss we suffered on 9/11. If terrorist atrocities were enough to discredit a cause, the Palestinians would have lost their constituency in the Muslim world decades ago. For many in the Muslim world, the burning towers of the World Trade Center represent a victory, not an atrocity, and the more we remind them of the suffering and pain of 9/11, the higher we raise the reputation of the man who inflicted that suffering and pain upon us.

Nor will we make much of an impact by denouncing terrorist attacks as "un-Islamic." Obviously, it would be helpful and encouraging if some important Islamic authority were to condemn such attacks in unequivocal terms. But since few or none of them have done so, it is worse than futile for a Christian American president to do it.

The future of extremist Islam will be decided by Muslims themselves, by reference to their own values and their own interests. We do have it in our power, though, to encourage a reassessment of those interests—and to promote more enlightened versions of those values than those that seem to predominate now.

Wherever people of Islamic culture are struggling with the difficulties of the transition to the modern world, the missionaries of militant Islam have gone forth, often financed by Saudi money, to promise that Islamic law and holy war will ease their poverty and salve their pride. In the last chapter, we argued that we should apply every possible pressure to halt Saudi Arabia's campaign to spread its murderous version of Islam—including, if necessary, encouraging the secession of the kingdom's oil-producing Eastern Province.

Yet even if the Saudis were to end their aid tomorrow, they have already disseminated their creed, and it has taken its evil root. Nigeria, for example, is a constitutionally secular republic, whose population is divided evenly between Muslims and non-Muslims. Yet since January 2000, seven of

Nigeria's northern states have imposed Sharia law on their people. Under Sharia, penalties for crimes against non-Muslims are less severe than penalties for crimes against Muslims, the testimony of non-Muslims can be disregarded altogether in a case against a Muslim, the testimony of women is worth half that of men, theft is punished by maiming, and sexual offenses are punished by flogging and stoning. Anti-Christian pogroms keep erupting in Nigerian cities. The whole world heard about the November 2002 riot sparked by a newspaper column that mocked Muslim objections to the Miss World contest. That riot in the city of Kaduna killed 215 people and destroyed twenty churches and ten thousand homes. Horrible as it was, it was by no means the bloodiest sectarian battle in Nigeria's recent history. Out of dozens of possible examples, here are just three:

In February 2000, Christians peacefully protesting the introduction of Sharia law in Kaduna state were attacked by a Muslim mob. In the ensuing fighting, *two thousand* people were killed.

Twenty-two thousand people in Baluchi state lost their homes in a July 2001 riot. The riot started when a non-Muslim woman refused a bus driver's order to sit apart from the men.

In October 2001, news of the American air strikes in Afghanistan provoked a Muslim mob in the important city of Kano to rampage through the small Christian quarter. Two hundred people were killed. The rioters carried posters of Osama bin Laden.

Nor is Nigeria unique. In Indonesia, a country once famous for its easygoing, syncretic version of Islam, Saudi-inspired extremists have launched wars against their Christian neighbors in Sulawesi and the Maluku islands, with the explicit intention of eliminating the Christian population altogether. There are no statistics on the number killed, but they certainly number in the thousands. Hundreds more have apparently been forced to convert to Islam to save their lives or the lives of their children. Homes and churches have been destroyed and a Christian university sacked.

Pakistan's founders had hoped to build a secular state with a Muslim identity—a state that was culturally Muslim in the way that India is culturally Hindu, but with a civil code, a secular education system, and tolerance for religious minorities. The country's founder, Mohammed Ali Jinnah, said, "I would rather be protector-general of the rights of the Hindu minority in Pakistan than governor-general of Pakistan. You will find in the course of time Hindus would cease to be Hindus and Muslims would cease to be Muslims, not in the religious sense, because that is the personal faith of each individual, but in the political sense, as citizens of the state." Jinnah's enlightened ambitions have been blasted by a lethal combination of Pakistani poverty and Saudi wealth. Pakistan's aspirations to educate all its citizens have failed miserably. Saudi charities have stepped into the gap, building a network of some six thousand religious colleges that teach their (male-only) students to memorize the Koran in its original Arabic—and to interpret the Koran in the light of the ideology of jihad.

The Pakistani military, once the guardian of the state's founding traditions, has struck its own devil's bargain with the Saudis. The Saudis footed most of the bill for the Pakistani nuclear bomb and contributed heavily to the costs of the guerrilla campaign against the Soviets in Afghanistan. In the process, they imbued both the security services and to a lesser degree the army itself with the Saudi brand of intolerant Islam. In 1979, Pakistan's then military ruler, Muhammad Zia ul-Haq, instituted Sharia courts for religious offenses, starting a process of Islamicization that culminated in 1991 when Sharia was declared the supreme law of Pakistan, over and above even the constitution. Pakistan midwifed the creation of the Taliban and actively supported its takeover of neighboring Afghanistan. Thousands of Pakistanis fought for the Taliban against the United States—and in December 2001, Pakistani intelligence surreptitiously helped them to escape capture by the United States. Both the American journalist Robert Sam Anson and the French philosopher Bernard-Henri Lévy, in the course of separate investigations into the murder in Pakistan of *Wall Street Journal* reporter Daniel Pearl, became convinced that, at a minimum, Pearl's kidnapping occurred with the acquiescence of important elements of the Pakistani secret services—possibly as a warning to Pakistan president Pervez Musharraf of their ability to cause trouble if he drew too close to the United States.

In the Arab heartland of Islam, the intellectual lights are dimming before our eyes. Despite its colossal oil wealth and the lavishly funded universities in the Persian Gulf, the Arab world produces virtually zero scientific papers and patents. A 2002 United Nations report on the condition of the Arab world observed that the nations that constitute the Arab League, total population more than three hundred million, annually translate about 330 books, one-fifth the number translated by Greece, population less than eleven million. But then the education system does not exactly stimulate demand for foreign books or ideas: One-third of the students at Saudi universities are enrolled in Islamic studies.

Morally, too, the Arab world is turning inward. Minorities are being driven out. Jewish populations were expelled and their property confiscated in the 1940s and 1950s. Since the 1970s, more subtle pressures have prodded the region's Christians to seek refuge in Australia, Canada, Europe, and the United States. There are now five times as many Lebanese Christians living outside Lebanon as live inside it. Iraq's Christian population has dropped from 6 percent of the total as recently as 1980 to less than 3 percent today. In 1975, Egypt was still one-fifth Coptic Christian. But to prove his Islamic credentials after the peace with Israel, Egypt's Anwar Sadat withdrew state protection from the Copts. At least one million Copts have emigrated since 1980; today the community makes up somewhere between 6 and 9 percent of the Egyptian population.

And whatever one's views of the merits of the Israeli-Palestinian dispute, the adulation in the Arab world of terrorist attacks on noncombatant Israelis, including children, is not the sign of a morally healthy society. After a Palestinian girl named Ayat Akhras detonated herself in a Jerusalem supermarket, killing two people and maiming twenty-five, the Saudi Arabian ambassador to London published a poem to honor her:

> Tell Ayat, the bride of loftiness . . .
> She embraced death with a smile . . .
> While the leaders are running away from death,
> Doors of heavens are opened for her.
>
> You [Ayat] died to honor God's word.
> [You] committed suicide?
> We committed suicide by living
> Like the dead.

The ambassador's celebration of murder is something new in the culture of the Arab Middle East. And as far as we can observe, it evokes no more condemnation or disapproval from his society than it would have among the ancient Aztecs or modern Nazis or any of the other death cults that have from time to time poisoned the human mind.

Confronted with such obdurate unreason, it may seem doubtful that other ideas can gain even a hearing, much less real influence. Yet we have seen many times how evil ideas that seemed to hold millions in their grip have yielded to new realities—or been smashed by unexpected defeats. So we must be on the lookout for ways to change the realities of the people now in the grip of extremist Islam, firmly trusting that they too are members of the same human family as are the peoples of all the other nations that have emerged from tyranny into freedom.

Democracy

"THE WORLD HAS a clear interest in the spread of democratic values, because stable and free nations do not breed the ideologies of murder. They encourage the peaceful pursuit of a better life." Those words of President Bush, delivered at the American Enterprise Institute on February 26, 2003, have startled and offended Americans and Europeans from across the political spectrum.

Here is Christopher Patten, a former minister in Margaret Thatcher's cabinet, now chancellor of Oxford University: "The argument is too crude. I start to worry about what Robespierre called armed missionaries . . . democracy at the point of a gun."*

And here is Jesse Jackson saying pretty much the same thing from the far left: "President Bush feels divinely 'called' to convert other countries' governments from oppressive regimes to democratically free governments. He is freeing Iraq through 'gunboat diplomacy,' then proposes to govern it with gunpoint democracy."†

The right-of-center journalist Robert Kaplan warns:

---

* Philip Stephens, "High Table Talk: The New Chancellor of Oxford University Tells Philip Stephens Why He Loves Dim Sum. And Rattling Neo-Conservative Cages," *Financial Times,* August 9, 2003, p. 12.

† Jesse L. Jackson, "America Exports Flawed Democracy," *Baltimore Sun,* April 13, 2003, p. 5-C.

"Democracy, in its early phases, is more likely to lead not to peace, but to demagogic politicians competing with each other over who can be more anti-American and more anti-Semitic."[*]

"The entire idea of an American-led democratic revolution in the Mideast has an air of fantasy about it," agrees left-of-center professor Paul Starr.[†]

Those who believe that the extremism that pervades contemporary Islamic culture might somehow be connected to the oppressiveness of Middle Eastern politics have been damned as "fanatics,"[‡] "crazy,"[§] and blinded by "hubris."[‖]

So who are these madmen who advocate greater democracy for the Middle East? They include the world's leading scholar of Islamic civilization, Bernard Lewis.[#] They include Paul Wolfowitz, deputy secretary of defense, who as assistant secretary of state for East Asia in the Reagan administration was the crucial figure in forcing from power *two* Pacific Rim

---

[*] Robert Kaplan, "Don't Try to Impose Our Values," *The Wall Street Journal*, October 10, 2001, p. A16.

[†] Paul Starr, "A War for Democracy?," *American Prospect*, April 1, 2003, p. 3.

[‡] William Pfaff, "Which Country Is Next?," *International Herald Tribune*, April 10, 2003, p. 8.

[§] Charley Reese, "Neoconservatives Are Crazy," King Features Syndicate, September 27, 2002.

[‖] David Corn, "The Hubris of the Neocons," TheNation.com, March 31, 2003, www.thenation.com/capitalgames/index.mhtml?bid=3&pid=532.

[#] William O. Beeman, "From Respected Scholar to Neoconservative Ideologue," *Providence Journal*, May 30, 2003, p. D9. Beeman, the director of Brown University's Middle East Studies Department and a scholar whom not everyone would describe as "respected," was especially incensed at Lewis's "outrageous" view that the United States should help Iranians liberate themselves from the rule of the ayatollahs, which he termed "attacks on the Islamic world."

dictators: Ferdinand Marcos of the Philippines in 1985 and Chun Doo Hwan of South Korea in 1986. Both countries are thriving democracies today. (For these and other services to world freedom and the American nation, Wolfowitz was accused of "harboring a 'passionate attachment' to a nation not our own" by the commentator Patrick Buchanan.)* They include former UN ambassador Jeane Kirkpatrick, who argued in the 1980s that democracy could come to the war zone of Nicaragua, El Salvador, Guatemala, and Honduras if communism was defeated—as indeed it has. They include Prime Minister Tony Blair of Great Britain, who told a joint session of Congress in July 2003 that "freedom, democracy, human rights, the rule of law . . . are not Western values, they are the universal values of the human spirit. And anywhere, anytime ordinary people are given the chance to choose, the choice is the same: freedom, not tyranny; democracy, not dictatorship; the rule of law, not the rule of the secret police."

Nobody thinks that it will be fast or easy to bring democracy to the Middle East. The democratizers understand the obstacles better than their critics. They have often devoted whole lifetimes to studying them. But they perceive something that the people who dismiss the democratizers fail to see: the poisonous cultural effect of tyranny.

Take a vast area of the earth's surface, inhabited by people who remember a great history. Enrich them enough that

* Patrick J. Buchanan, "Whose War?," *American Conservative*, March 24, 2003, available at www.amconmag.com/03_24_03/cover.html. The "nation not our own" to which Buchanan refers is neither the Philippines nor South Korea, but Israel.

they can afford satellite television and Internet connections, so that they can see what life is like across the Mediterranean or across the Atlantic. Then sentence them to live in choking, miserable, polluted cities ruled by corrupt, incompetent officials. Entangle them in regulations and controls so that nobody can ever make much of a living except by paying off some crooked official. Subordinate them to elites who have suddenly become incalculably wealthy from shady dealings involving petroleum resources that supposedly belong to all. Tax them for the benefit of governments that provide nothing in return except military establishments that lose every war they fight: not roads, not clinics, not clean water, not street lighting. Reduce their living standards year after year for two decades. Deny theme any forum or institution—not a parliament, not even a city council—where they may freely discuss their grievances. Kill, jail, corrupt, or drive into exile every political figure, artist, or intellectual who could articulate a modern alternative to bureaucratic tyranny. Neglect, close, or simply fail to create an effective school system—so that the minds of the next generation are formed entirely by clerics whose own minds contain nothing but medieval theology and a smattering of third world nationalist self-pity. Combine all this, *and what else would one expect to create but an enraged populace ready to transmute every frustration in its frustrating daily life into a fanatical hatred of everything "un-Islamic"?*

This fetid environment nourishes the most venomous vermin in the Middle Eastern swamp. And the implicit answer of the antidemocrats—support the local authoritarian regimes as they stomp on their people, because the people are even nastier than the regimes—lost its credibility on 9/11. The lesson of 9/11 is this: The stomping isn't working anymore. The extremists have become too numerous, too powerful. And the governments of the Middle East are decreasingly willing to do our stomping for us. That's another lesson of 9/11: The old line between "extremist groups" and the "moderate governments" we could trust to control those extremists is getting blurrier by the month. As the extremists get stronger, their ideas infiltrate the region's governments—so while Saudi decision-makers may have been acting cynically when they acquiesced in al-Qaeda's plotting against the United States, those less senior Saudi princes who have supported al-Qaeda and Hamas may well have been perfectly sincere—as sincere, say, as those German aristocrats who supported Hitler before he came to power.

In the Middle East, democratization does not mean calling immediate elections and then living with whatever happens next. That was tried in Algeria in 1995, and it would have brought the Islamic extremists to power as the only available alternative to the corrupt status quo. Democratization means opening political spaces in which Middle Eastern people can express concrete grievances in ways that bring action to improve their lives. It means creating representative institutions that protect minorities and women in a part of the world where minorities and women very much need protection. It means deregulating the economy to create economic opportunities and also to reduce the government's control over its people's livelihoods. It means shrinking and reforming the Middle Eastern public sector so that it functions honestly and responsively. It means perhaps above all establishing schools that prepare young people for the world of today, not the world of 1,300 years ago.

A big job. The good news is, we've done it before—in Western Europe, in East Asia, and in Central America. That record suggests it is not hopeless to try it again. And since the alternative to trying is more of the same incitement and rage that killed three thousand Americans—we have to try.

The Power of Good Examples

EXTREMIST ISLAM OFFERS one answer to the problem of Arab political failure. Iraq presents an opportunity to offer another.

Saddam's terror drove a generation of Iraqi intellectuals and political leaders into exile. There they saw that almost every Arab political grouping supported their persecutor, sometimes for ideological reasons, sometimes because they had been bought, sometimes because they were afraid. The effect was to alienate many of the Iraqi exiles from the rest of the Arab world—and liberate them from its dogmas: not only Baathism, but also Marxism, Islamism, even nationalism. David Frum once asked an exiled Iraqi communist what he thought of Iraqi National Congress leader Ahmed Chalabi. "I think that he would not murder me for disagreeing with him." When Frum suggested that this was a pretty feeble compliment, the communist retorted, "Where I come from, it's a pretty *large* compliment." Kanan Makiya, a leading Iraqi American intellectual, champions the rights of Kurds and Assyrians—and again it is hard to think of any other Arab country that has produced thinkers who even acknowledge the existence of minorities, much less show any concern for their well-being. In the Kurdish country, the two secular Kurdish political parties have administered their share of the UN oil-for-food revenues with a competence and honesty unexampled elsewhere in the region.

Obviously Chalabi and Makiya and the secular Kurds do not represent the entire political spectrum in Iraq. But the very fact that such people exist at all is reason for hope, at a time when few other reasons for hope exist in the Muslim Middle East. There are Iraqis who want to build a democratic state, answerable to all its people; who understand the power of markets; who respect the rights of minorities and women; who believe in religious liberty—and uniquely in the Arab world, these people now have an opportunity to hold and wield political power. Will they succeed? We can't know—but we can know that if they do succeed, if they even *partially* succeed, they will set off a convulsion in Arab politics.

Again and again in the past hundred years, the accidents of war and geography have created controlled experiments in which freedom and tyranny could compete against each other side by side. In Europe there was Germany: free on one side, communist on the other—and any child could see which side had bananas and friendly police and which did not. In Asia there was North and South Korea, as well as Taiwan and mainland China: both times, one people under two systems, one system leading to prosperity and happiness, the other to poverty and oppression.

Now we have an opportunity to help the people of Iraq create such a contrast in the Arab world, and it is vital that we succeed.

We did not come to Iraq to stay. Our tasks are to build a new Iraqi army and police force—and fast; to encourage the rapid spread of economic activity—and fast; and to get Iraq's oil fields producing again to meet Iraq's needs—and likewise fast. But the job of identifying, trying, and punishing the henchmen of the old regime is for Iraqis to do. The job of writing a constitution for their country is theirs as well. We can offer advice. We can help them take steps toward a free market system to replace Saddam's kleptocratic command economy. We can train Iraqi soldiers to combat insurgencies while respecting human rights, as we have trained armies in the Philippines and Latin America. We did not come to Iraq to govern it. We came to Iraq to restore the *self*-government stolen from it by decades of tyranny.

It is for that reason that so many of us who advocated military action in Iraq supported the Iraqi National Congress and Ahmed Chalabi. Chalabi had assembled a coalition that represented all the major groupings in Iraqi political life—a provisional government that could have given us local partners from the very start. Chalabi's critics complained that the man had lived outside Iraq too long, that he did not have a political base in the country. But after thirty-five years of Baathist repression, *nobody* except Baathist thugs, Shiite imams, and Sunni tribal sheikhs had a political base in the non-Kurdish areas of Iraq. We had come to Iraq to liberate it from Baathism. We had zero interest in delivering power to the imams. And romantic as some might find the tribal sheikhs, they were not the men to govern a nation 70 percent of whose people lived in cities. Our choice was either to work with Chalabi or to rule Iraq ourselves—and unfortunately we backed ourselves into that second alternative.

It's not too late to fix our mistake: to help Iraq create a provisional government that can work with the United States to move rapidly to full self-rule. But if we are to repair our earlier error, we must at all costs avoid the potentially much more serious error of turning Iraq into a ward of the United Nations or the "international community." Once the international bureaucrats get their hands on a society, they never let go. They continue to rule Kosovo, Cambodia, Somalia, and Bosnia five and ten years after the conflicts in those states ended.

Iraq's fate would be worse still. Nobody or almost nobody in the international community wishes to see Kosovo, Cambodia, Somalia, or Bosnia fail. But many of Iraq's neighbors do wish to see the new Iraq state fail, wish it ardently, because a success in Iraq would be profoundly threatening to them. An Iraqi success would raise questions about the whole

Arab world: If Iraq can have a representative government, why not Egypt? If private enterprise can pump Iraq's oil without corruption and kickbacks while paying a handsome tax into the common treasury, why could it not do so in Kuwait or Saudi Arabia?

We suspect that many of our European friends would be delighted to leave the UN to administer Iraq's oil reserves for a long, long time, parceling out special deals in the same amiable way that the UN previously parceled out oil-for-food money: so much for France, so much for Russia, with the people of Iraq always an afterthought—a polite, multilateral form of colonial rule.

That's not the future for which Americans waged war in Iraq. Americans waged war to overthrow a menace to the United States and the world and to offer freedom to a suffering people, just as Americans have previously brought freedom to many of the same people who thought Iraqis unworthy of it. A distinguished French scholar of Islamic affairs, Gilles Kepel, delivered a lecture in Teheran shortly after U.S. and coalition forces liberated Iraq. In the question-and-answer session that followed, a young woman rose. "We Iranians have only one friend," she said. Kepel waited for her to thank the French government for its support. She continued: "It is the Americans. They liberated you French in 1945. Why do you oppose their liberating *us* now?"

It is always possible for people to abuse their freedom. Others have done so before the people of Iraq, and the decision will ultimately be theirs. But we have given Iraqis a chance to lead the Arab and Muslim world to democracy and liberty.

How will we know whether our policies in Iraq are working? We got one clue within days of the end of major combat operations in April: The Iraqi dinar began to rise against the U.S. dollar. This may be the first time in financial history that losing a war had positive effects for the loser's currency. Look next for Iraq to begin running a trade deficit; that will mean that Iraq is running a *capital surplus* or, in other words, that more investment is entering the country than leaving it. Look for the price of real estate in Baghdad and Basra to rise. Look for members of exiled families to begin trickling back home. Those will be the indicators that the people of Iraq have become convinced that tomorrow will be better than today.

Iraq does not have to attain perfection to challenge the region with the power of a better alternative. If Iraq's new legislature is freely chosen and has means to hold the executive to account, if its bureaucracy is generally honest and competent and its courts are fair, if Iraqis can engage in private business without harassment and favoritism, if Iraq's different communities can live without fear—then that is an achievement as impressive as anything the democratizers could hope for.

Foreign Investment and Free Trade

TANKERS CROWD THE waters of the Persian Gulf. The hotels and airports of the region are thronged with travelers. In the malls of Kuwait City and Riyadh you can buy Hermès bags, Starbucks coffee, Nike sneakers. You'd never know from the brand names how economically isolated the people of the Middle East really are.

Omit oil, and the whole Arab world together exports as much each year as does the single small country of Finland. Foreign investors shun the region. In a typical year, even miserable Africa attracts twice as much foreign investment as the entire Arab world, oil wealth and all. Put it another way: Of every investment dollar sent from the industrialized to the developing world, two cents is committed to the Arab countries. When it was founded in 1881, the stock exchange in the Egyptian city of Alexandria ranked among the most important exchanges in the world. Today, all the shares listed on the Egyptian stock exchange are worth less than one-fourth as much as the shares listed on the Mexican exchange. The Gulf oil states stand near the top of the world's trading nations. Yet astonishingly few Gulf Arabs have much contact with the outside world. The oil is pumped, piped, loaded, shipped, and sold by foreign workers, and the same is true for the goods the Gulf states import. In Kuwait, for example, expatriates from more than 150 nations do the country's trade; 92 percent of those Kuwaitis who hold jobs work for the government. Only three million of Saudi Arabia's fourteen million citizens are employed. When a young Saudi took a job as a bellhop at a hotel, he made the front page of *The New York Times*. While there are seven million foreigners living in Saudi Arabia, the government takes care to ensure that their ways do not influence the natives; meanwhile, fewer and fewer Saudis are leaving the kingdom to study in the West, as the government cuts back its subsidies to higher education.

Arab isolation has exacted a heavy economic cost. Algeria was only very slightly poorer than Portugal in 1960; today Portugal is three times richer than Algeria. Syria was a substantially wealthier country than South Korea in 1960; today, South Korea is more than five times richer. While people all over the rest of the planet have adjusted to global commerce and exchange, sometimes reluctantly but usually successfully, the peoples of the Middle East have closed in on themselves, falling further and further behind, becoming angrier and more suspicious the further they fall.

The United States has worked for years to persuade Egypt and other Middle Eastern countries to abandon the perverse economic policies that produce economic failure. We have not succeeded yet. But we can at least open *our* economy to exports from poor countries, so that those that do venture on reform reap its rewards.

Pakistan, for example, has become a major textile producer. The textile industry employs 3.5 million Pakistanis, about 60 percent of the total industrial labor force. But the United States bars foreign textiles from U.S. markets with an elaborate system of tariffs and quotas that bears especially hard on countries just joining the textile market—like Pakistan. To make matters worse, after 9/11 American companies fled the Pakistani market altogether, and Pakistani exports tumbled. Some forty-eight thousand textile workers lost their jobs. By the end of 2001, Pakistan ranked a low twenty-first among textile exporters to the United States. It would have been wise to offer Pakistan immediate trade concessions after 9/11 to soften the blow of the economic catastrophe, but

Congress balked. Yet the long-run solution to Pakistan's problems is not a bigger textile quota, but a true free market in textiles, food, and other products, so that Pakistanis, Bangladeshis, and others, non-Muslims as well as Muslims, can earn their way to prosperity. Nor is this an imperative only for the United States: Bad as the U.S. record is on food and textiles, it positively gleams alongside the truly appalling shortsightedness and destructiveness of European trade policy.

Foreign investment may do even more good than foreign trade. In 1997, Islamic extremists attacked Egypt's tourism industry by massacring almost seventy visitors, most of them Swiss, at the ancient temples of Luxor. The year before, terrorists had killed eighteen Greek visitors. Those Egyptians who work in the hospitality industry were aghast. "If we found the terrorists, we would tear them apart, bit by bit," a waiter at a Luxor hotel told CNN.* If we could reinforce that waiter with hundreds of thousands more Egyptians who grew fruits and vegetables for the European market—or earned their living at the local offices of Citibank or Lloyd's—or assembled Dell computers—or loaded and unloaded ships at a thriving port of Alexandria—the terrorists would find their constituency slipping away.

Women's Freedom

TINA ISA WAS a sixteen-year-old daughter of Palestinian immigrants. The Isa family settled in St. Louis, Missouri, where

---

* www.cnn.com/WORLD/9711/18/egypt.attack.mubarak.

Tina enrolled in the local public schools. There she made the mistake of befriending a black boy. On November 6, 1989, Tina returned home from a date with the boy. As she entered the home, Tina's mother grabbed and held her. Her father then stabbed her to death: thirteen stabs in eight minutes. To the daughter's pleas for mercy, the mother barked, "Shut up!" and the father screamed over and over again, "Die, my daughter, die! Die! Die quickly! Die, my little one!"

We know all this because the Isa house was wiretapped by the FBI. Isa was an important figure in the U.S. operations of Abu Nidal's terrorist network, against which the FBI was building a case. Indeed, had the FBI not been wiretapping, it's doubtful that Isa would ever have been convicted of his crime. Both he and his wife testified that the daughter had attacked *them*—and local Muslim American associations promptly rallied to the defense of yet another Arab man supposedly singled out for prosecution only because of his name and ethnicity.

Tina Isa's murder is the kind that goes by the name *honor killing:* the murder by the men in the family of a female relative who has overstepped the rules that define female chastity. Honor killing is not, of course, an Islamic invention, but it remains astonishingly prevalent in the Islamic world. Pakistan's main human rights body counted 461 honor killings in that one country in the year 2002.*

Saudi Arabia's religious police, the *mutawwai'in,* hold the

---

* www.cnn.com/2002/WORLD/asiapcf/south/12/11/pakistan.women.

distinction of committing the Islamic world's first preventive honor killing. In March 2002, a fire swept through a girls' academy in Riyadh. Because Saudi Arabia systematically underinvests in girls' education, 800 girls were crammed into a building meant for 250. To prevent the girls from slipping out during the day, all the doors were locked. When the fleeing girls at last reached the school's one open exit, they were met by religious policemen who clubbed them back into the flames: The girls had not paused to pull themselves into their *abayas* and headscarves before fleeing, so they were violently barred from leaving the building. Fifteen girls were trampled or burned to death as a result, and fifty-two others were seriously injured. None of the religious policemen were punished.

Whenever militant Islam approaches power, it turns its wrath on women. During the Algerian civil war of the mid-1990s, Islamists tossed acid into the faces of the unveiled. Kashmiri Islamic militants issued a threat to do the same in 2001, frightening thousands of Kashmiri women into burqas. In the West, too, honor killings are proliferating. In February 2002, a Swedish Muslim woman was killed by her father for attempting to marry a man not of his choosing, the latest in a series of such crimes in Sweden. Honor killings have been reported in Denmark and Britain, too. Indeed, Muslim concepts of sexual morality are beginning to govern the lives of non-Muslim women in Western Europe. In September 2001, the Norwegian newspaper *Dagbladet* reported that two-thirds of the country's rapes were committed by people of non-Norwegian descent, almost all of them Muslim. A (woman) professor at the University of Oslo who was asked to comment on the report argued that "Norwegian women must take their share of responsibility for these rapes," because they dress in ways that Muslim men find provocative. "Norwegian women must realize that we live in a multicultural society and adapt themselves to it."*

Those who mocked President Bush for explaining that terrorists attacked the United States because they hate American freedom should consider the remark from the point of view of America's—and the world's—women. For the terrorists *do* hate the freedom of our women, not least because they fear it is putting ideas into the heads of *their* women.

As long as the battle raged in Afghanistan, the Bush administration made an issue of the status of women in Muslim lands. But now that the Taliban are gone, we hear much less about this issue. That is wrong. The oppression of women in contemporary Islamic culture sustains and exacerbates the extremism that produces terror—and women who seek emancipation from their oppression could constitute powerful forces for peace and freedom inside the Islamic world.

Women's oppression contributes to terror in the following ways:

1. A society that treats women like slaves will teach its men all the cruelty and violence of the slaveholder. On a visit to

* Bruce Bawer, "Tolerating Intolerance: The Challenge of Fundamentalist Islam in Western Europe," *Partisan Review,* March 2002, available at www.bu.edu/partisanreview/archive/2002/3/bawer.html. Bawer is an American expatriate living in Norway.

an Iranian family, journalist Geraldine Brooks was startled to watch a girl as young as six put to work making bread—and then to see the girl's slightly older brother rush into the room and laughingly snatch the fresh-baked bread from her hands and shove it into his mouth. He had already learned the first law of life in his society: He and those like him ruled; his sisters, his mother, even his elderly grandmother, must obey. In Saudi Arabia, women may not leave the house unless they are accompanied by a male family member; they may not leave the country without the permission of their father, husband, son, or even grandson, depending on who happens to be their nearest living male relation. We can well imagine what this kind of treatment does to the slave. Here is Alexis de Tocqueville's description of what it does to the master: "The citizen of the Southern states becomes a sort of domestic dictator from infancy; the first notion he acquires in life is that he is born to command, and the first habit which he contracts is that of ruling without resistance. His education tends, then, to give him the character of a haughty and hasty man, irascible, violent, ardent in his desires, impatient of obstacles, but easily discouraged if he cannot succeed in his first attempt."* Naguib Mahfouz, the greatest of living Arab novelists, has brutally portrayed the "culture of command" inside the Arab family—it is this culture that inflates the pride of the Islamic extremists to

* Alexis de Tocqueville, *Democracy in America* (vol. 1), trans. Philip Bradley (Alfred A. Knopf, 1980), p. 394.

the point where the failure of their society to keep pace with the achievements of the non-Muslim West becomes not a problem to be solved, but an insult to be washed out in blood.

2. Ignorance is the incubator of fanaticism—and a society in which women are kept ignorant will be a society in which everybody is kept ignorant. Illiterate mothers cannot teach their own children to read; so, uncoincidentally, societies marked by unusually high female illiteracy rates suffer high rates of male illiteracy as well. If, like the Saudis, you are determined to deny secular knowledge to your young women, you will soon discover—as the Saudis have done—that the only effective way to do so is to deny it to your young men as well.

3. Jobless young men in any culture do not find it easy to get married, and in a culture where sex outside of marriage is punishable by flogging or stoning, it should not surprise anyone that high unemployment rates produce lots of tense, angry young men. And since 1990, the unemployment rate in the Arab world has been very, very high: 25 percent in Saudi Arabia, for example. Much of this Saudi Arabian unemployment is voluntary. The government has an ambitious program of incentives to encourage Saudi employers to hire locals in place of the country's seven million foreign contract workers, but the locals turn up their noses at the jobs on offer. Still, voluntary or not, the social and sexual frustrations of unemployment may explain much of the fury that Muslim radicals direct

toward women who dress too temptingly—and it may
also explain the eagerness with which they seize on emotionally intense distractions, like terrorism.

4. Frustration may also go far to explain the militants' hatred of the West. In Islamic culture, as Bernard Lewis re-
minds us, Satan is perceived as a tempter—and the United
States is the greatest Satan because it is the greatest
tempter. "There are two kinds of internet cafe in the Middle East," reports one of *The Guardian*'s correspondents:
"Those where you sit with your back to the wall, and
those where you don't. The importance of these seating
arrangements should not be underestimated: having your
back to the wall means nobody can look over your shoul-
der to check what you are up to. In other words, it is a dis-
creet way of signaling that the cafe has a laid-back
attitude towards pornography." Some cafés discreetly
erect partitions between the computer screens; when
Yemen banned such devices in June 2002, half the Internet
cafés in the capital city went bankrupt overnight. The
most pornography-friendly café the journalist visited was
in Beirut; it was operated by supporters of Hezbollah.*
Imagine the emotions with which a devout, frustrated
young man would slink out of such a place afterward:
shame for himself, fury at the anonymous Westerners who
had tempted him, contempt for the civilization that cre-

* Brian Whitaker, "Islam at the Electronic Frontier," *The Guardian*, August 11,
2003, www.guardian.co.uk/elsewhere/journalist/story/0,7792,1016428,00.html.

ated the filth he had enjoyed, envy of the society in which the filth was freely available in the privacy of one's own bedroom.

5. Where women have possessed political power, they have been bulwarks against social conflict and ideological radicalism. It was not just egalitarian sentiment that prompted American occupation authorities to insist that liberated France (1944), Italy (1945), and Japan (1947) grant women the vote. The occupiers were well aware that male voters in those countries favored the communists, while women overwhelmingly preferred more conservative parties. Robert Kaplan's apprehensions that greater democracy would transform elections into bidding wars between anti-American demagogues might subside a little if women were allowed to vote in those elections on the same terms as men.

So how do we advance the cause of female emancipation in the Muslim world?

Where governments are open to the notion and where we have leverage, American money and technical assistance can encourage women's education and employment. In Pakistan, for example, where three-quarters of women cannot read, the United States supports a UN program that pays parents to send their daughters to school. Every girl who attends a girls' academy for twenty days out of the month receives a four-liter can of edible oil at the end of every month. The oil-for-school program, if we can call it that, was launched in 2000;

in July 2003, 125,000 girls received the oil. Unfortunately, six million other Pakistani school-age girls (and two million boys) remain unenrolled altogether.

Where the United States lacks leverage, we should not shy away from deliberate, measured confrontation. Saudi Arabia, for example, is not a traditional, tribal society like rural Pakistan. It is in many ways quite a sophisticated place, enforcing an especially nasty system of segregation and control upon half its people. If apartheid in South Africa was our business, it is hard to see why Saudi oppression of women is not our business, even aside from the 9/11 connection. But the 9/11 connection is real, and it is the best warrant we could have to press the Saudis for change. The most logical place to begin is with the plight of those American women, wives or daughters of Saudi men, who are trapped inside Saudi Arabia at the whim of their fathers or—in many cases—the husbands to whom they have been forcibly married. Article 13 of the Universal Declaration of Human Rights grants "everyone" the "right to leave any country, including his own, and return to his country." Persistent Saudi violations of this right call out for publicity—and for an American response. In the 1970s, we responded to Soviet restrictions on emigration from the Soviet Union with the Jackson-Vanik trade sanctions. Nobody can impose trade sanctions on the world's largest oil exporter. But we could stir the pot in other ways—by, for example, requiring all air itineraries to Saudi Arabia to provide passengers with a printed warning of the risks to American women who relocate there or by recognizing Saudi

women as a class of people with a well-founded fear of per-
secution who ought to be eligible for asylum in the United
States.

The craving for liberty that Tony Blair described in his
speech to Congress exists in women, too. We need to remind
the women of Islam ceaselessly: Our enemies are the same as
theirs; our victory will be theirs as well.

A Solution in Palestine?

THE BRITISH COMEDY troupe Monty Python used to do a
sketch about a quiz show in which the answer to every question was the word *pork*. Many of our foreign policy "experts," especially Middle East "experts," seem to approach
the problems of the world in the same spirit. For them, the
answer to every question about world peace and security is
"a Palestinian state." Above all, they are confident that the
surest way to assuage the Arab and Muslim rage that produced 9/11 is with concessions to the Palestinians. On the eve
of the Iraq war, two former national security advisers, Zbigniew Brzezinski and Brent Scowcroft, published an op-ed
piece calling for the United States to announce its commitment to the swift creation of a Palestinian state in all or
nearly all of the West Bank and Gaza. Why should the United
States do that? What's in it for Americans? The former advisers offered this answer: An American commitment to create a
Palestinian state "would also facilitate international cooperation with the U.S. in its war on terrorism and in its efforts to

encourage democracy world-wide."* In other words—if we give the Palestinians what they claim to want, the Islamic world and the European countries will be somewhat more likely to cooperate with us than they otherwise would.

The authors of this book can see why the right kind of Palestinian state would be good for Palestinians and Israelis. A Palestinian democracy that had neither the means nor the desire to destroy Israel, that was able to maintain order and stop terrorism, that accepted demilitarization and renounced all claims to the territory of a secure and defensible Israel—such a Palestinian state would be a welcome member of the community of nations. But useful as such a state would be, its establishment will do little to save the United States from the war against terrorism that it must fight and win.

Men like Brzezinski and Scowcroft think otherwise. Their views, to one degree or another, are conventional wisdom within the foreign policy establishment in this country and even more in Europe. Here is their reasoning, as best we understand it:

For hundreds of millions of Muslims around the world, or so the conventional view holds, the plight of the Palestinians has become the most vivid of all examples of Muslim humiliation and defeat. The Palestinian problem excites resentment and anger that al-Qaeda and other extremist groups can exploit, and the inability of Arab and Muslim

* Zbigniew Brzezinski and Brent Scowcroft, "A 'Road Map' for Israeli-Palestinian Amity," *The Wall Street Journal*, February 13, 2003, available at ffip.com/opeds021303.htm.

governments to solve that problem discredits them in the eyes of their people. By bringing a Palestinian state into being, the United States would calm passions in the Muslim world, strengthen friendly Arab governments, and prove itself a friend of Muslim aspirations. Osama bin Laden may still want to destroy us—but he would cease to find so large a constituency.

This thinking is not completely wrong. *If* the United States were to denounce Israel as an illegal occupier of Muslim land, attack it, deport the Jewish population, and turn over the Temple Mount to the Palestinians, we might well enjoy some of the benefits listed above.

But the United States will not do any of those things. At most, the United States might use its influence to help broker the creation of a neutralized, disarmed Palestinian ministate on the West Bank and in Gaza, with its capital in a part of Jerusalem, under the leadership of a president untainted by extremism. Israel will still be powerful and rich. "Palestine" will be weak and poor. "Palestine's" narrow borders and its reduced sovereignty will constitute a painful, permanent monument to the most recent Arab defeat. The best deal that the Palestinians are likely to get from the Bush administration will certainly be no more attractive than the deal Yasser Arafat rejected at Camp David in September 2000. Years of war, thousands dead, the total ruin of the Palestinian economy—all for less than nothing.

Liberal-minded Americans and Europeans, with their professed compassion for the defeated and the downtrodden, imagine a Palestinian state as a means of alleviating the suffering and redressing the grievances of unhappy people. In the current conflict, Palestinian sympathizers stress the almost three-to-one disparity between Palestinian and Israeli casualties. But when studied, the numbers reveal a rather different message than they suggest at first: 55 percent of the Palestinians killed have been combatants or violent protesters; almost 80 percent of the Israelis killed have been noncombatants.*

The Arab and Islamic world, however, has never cared much about the suffering and grief of the Palestinians. If it had, Arabs and Muslims could not be so massively indifferent to Palestinian suffering and grief when they cannot be attributed to Israel. Richard Perle spent an evening in Riyadh in 1973 with a group of young Saudi officials. Among them was a young member of the royal family, Saud al-Faisal, then serving as deputy to the minister of oil. Today he is the Saudi foreign minister. The conversation continued well into the night. At one point, Faisal said, "You must understand our sympathy for the Palestinians."

Perle replied: "I was told your contribution to the Palestinians last year was under $20 million—for a country as rich as Saudi Arabia, that's not much sympathy; and besides, our experts think that most of that is to keep them quiet right here in Riyadh."

---

* The study was conducted by the International Policy Institute for Counter-Terrorism and is available at www.ict.org.il. It was most recently updated on May 21, 2003.

"Not most of it," he said. "All of it."*

Sadly, there is no Arab country except Jordan in which Palestinians are permitted to become citizens, hold passports, own land, or send their children to the local schools. Lebanon forbids most Palestinians to enter seventy-two different professions, including law and medicine, and denies them access to the public health system. Kuwait expelled its three hundred thousand Palestinian residents in 1991 as a collective punishment for collaborating with the Iraqi invasion. Many of these individuals had lived in Kuwait for decades; virtually all of them were innocent of any wrongdoing; yet their dispossession provoked hardly a murmur of protest.

In the Arab and Muslim world, the Palestinian issue has never been about compassion, mercy, or even justice. First and always, the issue has been about vengeance. In the destruction of Israel and the reconquest of the Holy Land, Arabs and Muslims would at last salve the sting of their entire string of defeats stretching back to 1683. But to receive a piece of Palestine as a gift from the Americans and a grudging concession from the Israelis? That's charity, not revenge. Could this explain why Yasser Arafat spurned Bill Clinton's and Ehud Barak's offers at Camp David? Like Anwar Sadat, who could make peace with Israel only after he had won a tactical victory against the Israelis in October 1973, Arafat went to war in September 2000 hoping to bloody the Israelis

---

* If this ever comes to the minister's attention, he will almost certainly deny it. As readers might imagine, it was the sort of exchange a young Senate staffer does not easily forget.—RP.

enough to make his later acceptance of a deal look like a victory. But Sadat had the wisdom to seek a cease-fire before the Israelis destroyed his forces. Arafat failed to do so, and blow by blow, the Israelis annihilated his miniature army, his presidential palace, and his little fleet of limousines and helicopters, until he was left alone in the ruins of Fatah's headquarters in Ramallah.

The Palestinian state envisioned by President Bush may well improve the lives of the population of the West Bank and Gaza. Moderate Arab governments may well wish to seize on the creation of the ministate as justification for the belated resolution of a quarrel that has lasted far too long. But the extremists will up the ante on the moderates. They will denounce the ministate as a betrayal of the Palestinian cause. They will demand that every great-niece or third cousin whose family once lived on what is now Israeli territory must be allowed to return. Or they will demand the Western Wall. Or they will find some other pretext for refusing ever to make peace with Israel. And because the extremists have not yet been crushed—because they still possess more prestige and authority than many Arab governments—because the intellectual voices in the Arab world arguing for compromise, tolerance, liberty, and progress are so faint and timid—the Arab and Muslim populations, and even Arab and Muslim elites, are likely to heed the extremists, condemn the Israeli-Palestinian agreement, and demand the death of any Palestinian who signs it.

For these reasons, it is unlikely that such an agreement

will ever be negotiated or that the Palestinian leadership will ever be induced to accept it. When Michael Collins signed the Anglo-Irish treaty of 1921, he said sadly, "I fear I have signed my death warrant." He was assassinated within the year. No Palestinian leader has ever shown anything like the courage of a Michael Collins. There will be no signature. While one hopes otherwise, the likeliest result of the Bush administration's exercise in Israeli-Palestinian peacemaking will be another abject failure of the so-called peace process.

The Israelis, for their part, will accept no deal with the Palestinians that does not offer convincing security guarantees against terrorism. But the new Palestinian state will lack the power to issue or honor such guarantees unless Hamas, Islamic Jihad, and the other terror groups are destroyed beforehand. Hamas, most polls show, is more popular with ordinary Palestinians in the West Bank and Gaza than Fatah or any of the main-line Palestinian factions. So the new state will need help. From whom? There is one obvious candidate: the state's sponsor and creator, the United States.

In other words, if this new state comes into being before the terror groups are destroyed, it will require covert and overt American police and military support to defend itself against many of its *own people.* We will begin by showing the state how to fight its people. Soon, we will find we are helping it to fight its people. In the end, we will be fighting its people on its behalf. We will have created a Palestinian South Vietnam.

Since 1945, our planet has witnessed the birth of more than a hundred states and the movement of hundreds of borders. Those movements are seldom agreeable to everyone, but in the end nations accept them, on the grounds that a settled border is better than war. The Germans reconciled themselves to the loss of Prussia, and the Russians acknowledged the secession of Kazakhstan; Irish Catholics have adjusted themselves to being deprived of Ulster, and the Serbs are gradually coming to terms with the autonomy of Kosovo. In the third world, too, states have surrendered treasured aspirations rather than shed blood forever: Somalia gave up the Ogaden, Guatemala stopped demanding Belize, and the Indonesians eventually withdrew from East Timor. There is one glaring, conspicuous exception to this willingness to swallow disappointment, and that is the grim refusal of the Arab world to accept the verdict of half a dozen wars since 1948 and make peace with Israel. In the fifteen years after Israel declared its independence in 1948, it received twice as many refugees from Arab lands as the Arabs received from Israel. None of these Jewish refugees have ever staked a claim to the homes, farms, and companies that once belonged to them back in Algeria, Egypt, Iraq, Morocco, and Yemen. They resettled themselves in their new country and let go of the past. The exiled Palestinians should likewise be accepted as citizens of Arab countries in which they now live. The greatest—indeed, the sole—obstacle to peace is the feeling among many people in the Arab and Muslim world that anything that was once theirs can never legitimately be anybody else's. It would be as if the Greeks felt themselves entitled to blow up school buses in Turkey until the Turks returned Constantinople. The

Arab-Israeli quarrel is not a *cause* of Islamic extremism; the unwillingness of the Arabs to end the quarrel is a *manifestation* of the underlying cultural malaise from which Islamic extremism emerges.

We reiterate: A peaceful, open, and democratic Palestinian state would be a good thing in its own right and could well contribute to the stability of the region. But there should be no illusions: We will not cure the vast malaise in Muslim civilization exposed by 9/11 by carving out a twenty-third Arab state in the Judaean hills.

We write these words fully aware of how some readers and critics may react to them. According to the BBC's flagship documentary program, *Panorama,* a "small and unelected group of right-wingers . . . have hijacked the White House."* The members of this "close-knit" group, according to *BusinessWeek,* "have been called extremists, warmongers, American imperialists—and even a Zionist cabal."† They are, as an American contributor to the *New Statesman* helpfully points out, "unrepresentative" of "the U.S. population."‡ A writer for *The Nation* complained about the "reticence of almost all sides to broach the issue of Israeli and American Jewish influence on US foreign policy."§ This reticence did not

---

* news.bbc.co.uk/1/hi/programmes/panorama/3021001.stm.

† "Where Do the Neocons Go From Here?," *BusinessWeek,* May 12, 2003, available at www.businessweek.com/magazine/content/03_19/b3832081.htm.

‡ Michael Lind, "The Weird Men Behind George W. Bush's War," *New Statesman,* April 7, 2003, available at www.newamerica.net/index.cfm?pg=article&pubID =1189e.

§ Eric Alterman, "Can We Talk?," *The Nation,* April 3, 2003, available at www.thenation.com/doc.mhtml%3Fi=20030421&s=alterman.

inhibit Maureen Dowd of *The New York Times,* who has explained that the secretive "neocons" are motivated above all by a concern to "make sure it"—referring to American foreign policy—"is good for Ariel Sharon." *

The idea that world events are directed by a Jewish conspiracy is not exactly a novel one. But since 9/11, this ancient obsession has migrated from the intellectual and moral margins to form the central theme of much of the American and world media's reporting from Washington. Both of the authors of this book have spent many dozens of hours talking to journalists from around the world, almost all of whom eventually work their way up to the one big question: Is the war on terror a Zionist plot? The question is posed with beguiling directness by journalists from East Asia, with excruciating awkwardness by journalists from Germany, and with elegant sinuosity by journalists from Britain—but it is always asked.

As the ritualized murder of Daniel Pearl should remind us, we live in an era in which anti-Semitism is more rife than at any time since the 1930s. Jew-hatred is as essential to extremist Islam as it was to Nazism, and wherever extremist Islam takes root, from the suburbs of Paris to the bazaars of Paraguay, attacks on Jews soon follow. Jews and Judaism are for extremist Islam a unifying cause, a hatred that unites diverse and even quarreling subgroups.

Some Western governments, notably that of France, have hesitated to act to protect their Jewish populations against

---

* Maureen Dowd, "Neocon Coup at the Department d'État," *The New York Times,* August 6, 2003, p. A17.

attack—and have even denied that the attacks were occurring. This is not so much anti-Semitism as it is plain old political cowardice.

Nor do we think it is classical anti-Semitism that usually explains the global press's fascination with the myth of the neoconservative cabal in the halls of power in Washington.

Much of the rest of the world—and much of liberal opinion in the United States—decided sometime early in 2002 that it no longer wanted to fight the war on terror. Almost inevitably, the disheartened came to resent those who did want to keep fighting. Because of liberal opinion's persistent and pervasive disdain for President Bush, it simply could not accept that it was the president's determination that was pushing the war forward. Somebody else *had* to be responsible. Hence, the myth of the neoconservative cabal.

In the highly centralized and bureaucratic countries of Europe, it often is possible for a relatively small number of people to push through a plan or concept over the objections of most of the population. It's hard for many Europeans to appreciate that the United States does not operate like that: that, in fact, American policy is produced through representative institutions that cannot safely drift too far from public opinion.

Most important, the neoconservative myth offers Europeans and liberals a useful euphemism for expressing their hostility to Israel. Israel is everything that liberal Europeans think a state should not be: proudly nationalist, supremely confident, willing and able to use force to defend itself—

alone if need be. To such people, Israel is an ugly throwback to a past they wish to transcend. Israel is not the only such throwback, of course—but the others nearby (Russia, for example) are too dangerous to tangle with. Israel is big enough to look like a bully, but small enough to be pushed around. Those Americans who do not share this antipathy to Israel offend European sensibilities as much as if they owned a Hummer and dined exclusively on Big Macs. And the European media have obligingly depicted these unashamed supporters of Israel as sinister conspirators.

Perhaps these vicious misrepresentations are meant to salve the European conscience. For years, European governments have appeased and indulged terrorism. So long as Israel thrives by doing the opposite, the little state raises the question of whether the European stance is pragmatic and necessary—or fearful and dishonorable.

The joke is that for all the talk of how alien the neoconservatives supposedly are—for all the BBC's charming habit of pronouncing "Paul Wolfowitz" as "Paul Vulfuvitz," we suspect that the average Republican primary voter in, say, Kentucky thinks about foreign policy almost exactly as Washington's hawks do: that enemies cannot be palliated and must be fought. That sympathy of views, not conspiracy, explains why the advocates of a strong policy have prevailed since 9/11. The American public instinctively senses that in a dangerous world the toughest line is the safest line.

7. ORGANIZING FOR VICTORY

A NEW COMMITMENT to security at home; a new audacity in our strategy abroad; a new boldness in the advocacy of American ideals—all of this is essential to victory in the war on terror. But none of these grand efforts will achieve success unless we also overhaul the institutions of our government to ready them for a new kind of war against a new kind of enemy.

We are fighting the war on terror with the same people and the same bureaucracies that so conspicuously failed us on 9/11. In the summer of 2001, the Central Intelligence Agency received information that al-Qaeda was plotting to use aircraft as flying bombs against symbolic American targets.* The CIA passed the information to the Federal Bureau of Investigation. That same summer, the FBI office in Phoenix alerted the FBI national offices that an "inordinate number of

---

* U.S. Senate Select Committee on Intelligence and U.S. House Permanent Select Committee on Intelligence, Joint Inquiry into Intelligence Community Activities Before and After the Terrorist Attacks of September 11, 2001, S. Rept. No. 107-351, H. Rept. No. 107-792 (December 2002), p. 212.

persons of investigative interest" were enrolled at flight schools in Arizona.* The Minneapolis FBI office actually arrested one of these persons, Zacarias Moussaoui, and asked for permission to search Moussaoui's laptop computer. Permission was denied. The Minneapolis agent in charge of the Moussaoui case persisted: He was trying, he said, to make sure that Moussaoui "did not take control of a plane and fly it into the World Trade Center." He got back this answer from his superiors at the New York office: "That's not going to happen. We don't know he's a terrorist. You don't have enough to show that he's a terrorist. You have a guy interested in this type of aircraft—and that's it."[†]

That complacent reply from FBI New York epitomized the careless attitudes of an entire decade. The people who governed America in the 1990s now tell us that they were obsessed with the terrorist danger. At the time, they always seemed to have higher priorities. Yes, they wanted to prevent hijackings. But they wanted even more to protect the privacy rights of the likes of Zacarias Moussaoui. Yes, they wanted to track extremist groups. But they wanted even more to avoid singling out any one religious community. Yes, they wanted to track down and destroy terrorists. But not if it meant any actual fighting.

So at the very same time that it was claiming to be obsessed with the terrorist threat, the Clinton administration

* Ibid., p. 325.
† Ibid., pp. 323–24.

was piling restrictions upon the FBI and CIA. In 1995, the Clinton Justice Department prohibited the FBI from so much as clipping a newspaper article about an Islamic extremist group unless that group was the target of a specific investigation for a specific crime. Meanwhile, one of the CIA's agents in the Middle East, Robert Baer, was pulled from the region and threatened with prosecution under federal murder-for-hire statutes for attempting to organize a coup against Saddam Hussein.

Clues that connected one terrorist to another were frequently disregarded. New York prosecutors who investigated the 1990 killing of the extremist rabbi Meir Kahane insisted against the evidence that his murderer acted alone. In 1993, they discovered that Kahane's killer belonged to the same cell that tried to blow up the World Trade Center—but awareness of that earlier mistake did not prod investigators to follow the next round of clues linking the World Trade Center bombers to international terrorist organizations and foreign governments.

Ultimately, the blame for our failed terrorism policies of the 1990s belongs to the weak-willed leaders who could not muster the nerve for decisive action. But it's also true that leaders can fight only with the weapons available to them. In the war on terror, our weapons are our national security institutions. And the sad truth is that even months after 9/11, our institutions remain too often hunkered down in the vanished past, disturbingly unready for the work they must do.

In the early days after 9/11 there was much talk of the

need for "sacrifice." The sacrifice that is most urgently needed, however, is not a sacrifice of blood or money, but of discredited ideas and obsolete bureaucracies. Americans are asking their soldiers and sailors and marines, their intelligence officers, firefighters, police, and medics, to brave deadly risks. It is not too much to ask American political leaders to take on the established ways of Washington—and transform our national security institutions so that they can fight and win a war that started almost three years ago.

The transformation must begin with the single worst performer among those institutions: the FBI. But it must extend much farther: to the CIA, the armed forces, and, perhaps above all, the Department of State.

Nobody in the U.S. government, for example, has the job of tracking and catching terrorists wherever they may be found. The Central Intelligence Agency is supposed to track foreign threats. Should a terrorist elude the CIA and enter the United States, the CIA (if it has not lost the terrorist en route) is then supposed to hand responsibility to the Federal Bureau of Investigation, which is charged with defending Americans from domestic dangers. The division of labor between the two agencies was established when the CIA was established in 1947, at a time when all but the most privileged few had to cross the Atlantic by ship and when a three-minute transatlantic telephone call cost what most Americans would have considered a good day's pay. Perhaps the division worked well half a century ago; it certainly does not work well now.

The FBI is essentially a police force, and like all good police forces it goes to great lengths to respect the constitutional rights of the suspects it investigates. That is why the national FBI refused to authorize the search of Moussaoui's computer. But Moussaoui was not an American citizen under the protection of the American Constitution. He was not a criminal suspect. He is believed to have been a combatant in a hostile army, an army whose sole purpose was to commit atrocities against American civilians. A police force is inherently disabled in dealing effectively with someone like Moussaoui. And, ironically, the better the force—the more aware it is of the constitutional limits on police power, the more respectful of the rights of the accused—the more disabled it will be.

The FBI has tried to resolve the contradiction between crime fighting and counterterrorism by dividing itself in two: Most of the FBI chases traditional kinds of criminals with traditional police methods under the supervision of the regular courts. A small subsection of the Bureau, however, has been assigned the job of monitoring suspected terrorists under the supervision of a specially constituted secret antiterrorism court.

The strict rules imposed on the FBI in 1995 were intended to safeguard the division between criminal investigations and counterterrorism. Agents on the counterterrorism side were forbidden even to *talk* to people on the criminal side who might know something about their case. FBI agents could not visit a mosque to listen to the sermon, could not even tab extremist Web sites on their browsers, unless they were seeking information in a particular case. As Richard Clarke, the former chief of counterterrorism at the National Security Council, told the joint congressional committee, the FBI "didn't have the mission. It was not their job to be a domestic [intelligence] collection service. Their job was to do law enforcement. And they didn't have the rules that permitted them to do domestic intelligence collection." *

And even if the FBI had had the rules, it lacked the skills. As of 9/11, the FBI employed only twenty-one people who spoke Arabic well enough to penetrate Islamic extremist groups inside the United States.[†] Nor was the FBI keen to recruit people who already belonged to such groups. The congressional 9/11 inquiry found that "FBI Headquarters and field managers were often unwilling to approve potentially controversial activity involving human sources who were in a position to provide counterterrorism intelligence. . . . The agent responsible for the source had to obtain approval from FBI Headquarters and the Department of Justice to allow the source to engage in illegal activity. According to FBI personnel, this was a difficult process that sometimes took as long as six months."[‡] Since the people most in the know about terrorism were of course up to their eyeballs in illegal activity, the FBI's own reluctance to employ them amounted in effect to an internal ban on recruiting counterterrorist sources.

Critics often describe the Patriot Act enacted after 9/11 as if it were coauthored by Joseph Stalin and Tomás de Torque-

* Ibid., p. 37.
† Ibid., p. 94.
‡ Ibid.

mada, but those same critics are notably vague when it comes time to describe what the law actually does. No wonder: If they ever offered details, their audience would be startled by how reasonable the law is—and how lax the critics would wish the law to be.

Before the Patriot Act, there was no federal law to determine when criminal suspects' e-mail could legally be intercepted and read. The Patriot Act did set a standard—exactly the same standard that governs the wiretapping of telephones. Federal law had simply missed the e-mail revolution. It missed the mobile phone revolution too: Before the Patriot Act, prosecutors had to get a separate warrant for *each hand-set* a terrorist suspect might possibly use. All a suspect had to do to throw prosecutors off his or her trail was switch to a new device. The Patriot Act allows judges to issue just one roving warrant, which follows the suspect wherever he or she happens to go.

The Patriot Act overrides the Clinton-era rules that denied information about terrorist activities garnered by intelligence means to police and prosecutors. For example, the FBI counterterrorism unit had for years possessed information that linked University of South Florida professor Sami al-Arian to the Palestinian terrorist group Islamic Jihad. Yet none of this information could be used, or even divulged, enabling al-Arian to be received at the Clinton White House and the pre-9/11 Bush White House as an honored representative of the American Muslim community. Al-Arian's son was hired onto the staff of Congressman David Bonior, and respected members of the Washington Republican establishment lobbied to halt the deportation of al-Arian's alleged co-conspirator, his illegal immigrant brother-in-law, Mazzan al-Najjar. It was the powers contained in the Patriot Act that enabled federal prosecutors to hit al-Arian with a fifty-one-count indictment and at last eject al-Najjar from the country.

The Bush administration is working hard to integrate an unruly gaggle of emergency and preparedness organizations into the new Department of Homeland Security. But even the best efforts of the Bush administration have taken us only so far. The Department of Homeland Security lost the battle to wrest control of domestic counterterrorism operations from the FBI. The domestic war on terrorism is being waged by the same people who so dismally mishandled it in the 1990s. They tell us they have mended their ways. Let us all hope so.

The CIA did not "have the mission" either. The CIA *is* an information collection and analysis agency, but not always a very good one. America's amazing technology allows us to gather immense quantities of data. But that data yields useful information only if it is analyzed without ideological prejudices or institutional biases. A good intelligence analyst must constantly question his own ideas about the phenomena he studies. Alas, the CIA does not live up to this standard. Over time, it has become an agency with very strong, mostly liberal policy views, and these views have again and again distorted its analysis and presentation of its own information.

Since 1998, the CIA has focused intense attention on the al-Qaeda terrorist organization. But until 9/11, it paid astonishingly little attention to the larger trend of which al-Qaeda was a part: the rise of radical Islam. It is as if the intelligence services of the 1930s had studied Adolf Hitler as if he and his henchmen were a small gang of lunatics—and ignored the enormous mobs that cheered and followed them.

The CIA is generally good at counting things. If a president wants to know how much gold South Africa mined last year or how many intercontinental ballistic missiles China can fire, the CIA can tell him. But this very skill tends to blind the CIA to things that cannot be counted: religious fervor, for instance. The CIA is blinded, too, by the squeamishness that many liberal-minded people feel about noticing the dark side of third world cultures.

The CIA got terrorism wrong in much the same way— and for many of the same reasons—that it got the Soviet Union wrong during the cold war. The CIA's analysts could not emancipate themselves from the ideologically liberal assumptions they brought with them from their elite colleges: that the Soviet Union was a more or less normal state with a more or less effective economy; that we could allay its hostility through diplomacy; that hopes for victory in the cold war were dangerous delusions. As a result, the analysts recoiled from reporting any facts that would have demanded a forceful U.S. response to the Soviets.

Ideology biased the people who staffed the CIA in favor of arms control agreements—and that bias, in turn, inhibited the agency from acknowledging evidence that the Soviets were cheating on their agreements. Richard Perle remembers a lengthy argument about whether some Soviet missile launchers at a missile test facility were "operational," in which case they would have pushed the Soviets over the maximum number allowed them by treaty, or merely "test launchers," in which case they would not. The debate raged for months. It was an issue that should have been settled easily. We had directly observed the Soviets treating the controversial missiles according to the standard operating procedure for genuine, operational, aimed-at-America missiles. The CIA clung to its view, offering ever more preposterous excuses for the Soviet position. At one point CIA personnel argued that the Soviets were acting out of habit, absentmindedly treating the missiles as operational even though they were not. Only very slowly and reluctantly did the CIA give way to reality.

Second, and even more seriously, the agency's liberal instincts blinded it to signs of the weakness of the Soviet economy. National security experts spent a lot of time back in the 1980s arguing over the size of the Soviet military budget. In these debates, the CIA kept insisting that Soviet economic statistics could basically be trusted, after certain adjustments were made. The Soviet economy, the CIA reported, was only slightly smaller than Japan's and growing fast.* The CIA therefore concluded that the Soviets were spending no more than 13 percent of their gross domestic product on their military forces; for many years the Agency refused to counte-

* The CIA's last cold war estimate of the East German economy, published shortly before the Berlin Wall came down, put East German GDP per capita at near parity with that of West Germany!

nance any figure over 9 percent. This was a hugely important statistic. If the Soviets were spending as little as one tenth of their output on their forces, it was reasonable to fear that without arms control treaty ceilings they would build even more weapons than they were already building. But if the Soviets were spending a higher percentage, it would be difficult if not impossible for them to build more. And if the Soviets could not build more, arms control agreements were wholly unnecessary, and potentially even harmful to the United States, since they committed us to surrender weapons we *could* afford to build in exchange for the Soviets surrendering additional weapons they could *not* afford to build.

The CIA kept insisting that the Soviets could afford to increase military spending dramatically right up to the moment when Soviet military spending broke the Soviet economy and the Soviet Union collapsed—at which point we learned that the Soviet statistics in which the CIA had trusted were worthless. The Soviets had been spending some 35 percent of their annual economic output on their military, more than double the CIA's highest-ever estimate and nearly four times the CIA's estimate through most of the final years of the cold war.

The CIA's miscalculations helped the Agency win some internal bureaucratic battles but caused it to miss entirely the sounds of the cracking and crumbling of the whole Soviet system. Ronald Reagan understood the performance and potential of the Soviet economy far better than the CIA. In a speech to the British House of Commons in 1983, he publicly predicted communism's imminent collapse. And he embarked on a strategy of challenging the Soviets that would have made little sense if they had had the economic vitality and potential on which the CIA insisted.*

The CIA's reports on the Middle East today are colored by similar ideological biases—exacerbated by poor understanding of the region's culture and a politically correct disinclination to acknowledge unflattering facts about non-Western peoples.

Like the FBI, the CIA employs few analysts who speak Arabic or Farsi, and fewer who understand the Middle East's culture and values. The CIA has sent agents to Egypt and Jordan who could not speak Arabic and at one point placed a man in charge of Iran who knew not a word of Farsi and whose errors destroyed our entire network in the country; the CIA then promoted him. When the regime of the shah of Iran began to crumble in the late 1970s, the administration of President Jimmy Carter engaged in a furious debate over the nature and character of the shah's challenger, the Ayatollah Ruhollah Khomeini. Many Carterites had convinced themselves that Khomeini was a kind of Iranian Desmond Tutu—a third world religious leader expressing legitimate discontents in spiritual language. Carter's UN ambassador, Andrew Young, even suggested that Khomeini was a man who "would eventually be hailed as a saint."

The CIA could have played a role in settling this im-

---

* There were those who estimated the Soviet defense burden more accurately: Harry Rowen, William Lee, Charles Wolf, and some others. But their views were largely ignored by the Agency.

mensely important controversy. As the crisis in Iran intensified, our country's most distinguished expert on the Islamic world, Professor Bernard Lewis of Princeton, translated excerpts from Khomeini's most recent book and edited them into an article for the op-ed page of *The New York Times*. As Lewis saw it, there was no reason for anyone in Washington to be baffled by Khomeini's views: They were available to read between hard covers. The editors of the *Times* sent Lewis's piece to Khomeini's spokesmen in Paris for comment. Khomeini's office angrily denounced the book as a forgery—and since Khomeini's followers around the world had been instructed to remove copies of the ayatollah's embarrassingly revealing book from library shelves, original copies were becoming scarce.

Lewis mentioned the problem to Richard Perle. Perle in turn sent Lewis's copy of the book over to the CIA with a request that the Agency authenticate it for the *Times*. The Agency refused: A CIA spokesman told Perle that nobody at Langley had ever seen the book before. Not only had the people we employed to help us understand what was going on in Iran failed to *read* Khomeini's book, they were even unaware that he had *written* it. And all of this at a moment when the future alignment of Iran was hanging in the balance.* At about this time, one of America's great strategic thinkers, Professor Albert Wohlstetter, planned a visit to Iran to inspect

---

* After the revolution, Khomeini's "little green book" would be reissued in millions of copies. By then even the Carterites did not need a book to understand the kind of man Khomeini was.

the volatile situation. Wohlstetter asked then CIA director Stansfield Turner whether we had an experienced, knowledgeable station chief in Teheran. Turner assured him that we did—although Turner could not recall the man's name. Still, a meeting was arranged, and Wohlstetter was greeted by the top CIA officer in Iran—a man who had only just arrived from Japan. The officer was fluent in Japanese, was, indeed, an expert on Japanese haiku poetry. But he had no experience in Iran and spoke no Farsi.

The record continues: The CIA maintained that Saddam Hussein would not invade Kuwait in 1991. Evidence of Iraq's mobilization was, the Agency thought, a feint, a device for putting pressure on the Kuwaitis to make concessions at the negotiating table. By the time the CIA realized what was going on, it was too late to take timely deterrent action. Then, after the Gulf War ended, we learned that the Agency had almost entirely overlooked Iraq's advanced nuclear weapons program. There is no record that anyone responsible for any of these faulty assessments was ever fired or even reassigned.

Partly as a result of the CIA's limitations, it has come to depend heavily on the information provided to it by Middle Eastern intelligence services, whose personnel do speak the language. Because of that dependence, the Agency often disapproves of U.S. actions that might threaten those services' willingness to cooperate with the United States. Since the most repressive governments tend to have the most knowledgeable services, it is the opinions and wishes of the very worst Arab governments that have the greatest influence within the CIA. That is one reason why the CIA in the 1990s objected so strenuously to talk of "democratizing" Iraq. (As the Iraqi National Congress bitterly joked, "The CIA wants a Saddam with a different mustache.") Few Arab governments felt much affection for Saddam, but elections in Iraq would constitute a clear and present danger to every king, emir, and president-for-life from Gibraltar to the Strait of Hormuz. Not a single one of the twenty-two heads of state in the Arab League was elected to his office; the first democratic president of Iraq will be only slightly less distasteful to the Arab League than would the first Jewish one.

The CIA's practice of working through Arab intelligence services explains the strange alliance that has sprung up since 9/11 between the CIA and the government of Syria. The doctrines that President Bush has enunciated since the terrorist attacks unmistakably mark Syria as an enemy of the United States. Syria has a long history of support for terror groups, and that support continues to this day. Syria possesses weapons of mass destruction, principally poison gas but also very probably biological agents as well. The Syrians provided weapons of war to Iraq in the months leading up to the U.S. campaign, and may have provided refuge to fleeing officials of Saddam's government.

According to the CIA, however, Syria has been helpfulness itself in the war on terror. Syria even took custody of some al-Qaeda suspects who had the bad luck to carry Syrian passports and shared with the United States at least some of the information obtained by means of Syria's famously vigorous techniques of interrogation. Many in the CIA were so delighted by the brutal Syrian dictatorship's sudden apparent cooperativeness that some unnamed CIA agents went so far as to complain to *New Yorker* correspondent Seymour Hersh in the summer of 2003 about Defense Department officials who threatened the relationship by harping on unpleasant- nesses like Syria's terrorist ties.* It's hard to know what about this story was most astonishing: the CIA's complaints themselves or the eagerness of Seymour Hersh, onetime hero of the far Left, to relay those complaints. We do not remem- ber him being so sympathetic to the Agency's cold-blooded realism when it wanted to work with the Guatemalan dicta- torship against Central American communists.

There are obvious dangers in collaborating with foreign intelligence services whose governments have interests funda- mentally opposed to our own. Clearly they cannot be trusted to share anything that it is not in their interest for us to know. They will mislead us when it is convenient for them to do so, which is all too often. During the cold war, the KGB often manipulated the CIA by feeding it misinformation through allegedly "independent" Eastern bloc intelligence services like Romania's. Today, it is likely to be Jordanian, Saudi, or Egyptian intelligence whose views influence CIA assessments of the region.

From Nathan Hale to William Casey, America's great spies have been individualists, eccentrics even, the very oppo- site of bureaucrats. And in its great days, the CIA was the

---

* Seymour Hersh, "The Syrian Bet," *The New Yorker,* July 28, 2003, p. 32.

very opposite of a bureaucracy. But over the past three decades, the CIA has ossified. In the 1970s, the CIA was buffeted by a series of scandals, which prompted Congress to impose new limits on the Agency's freedom of action. These reforms receive much of the blame for the drying up of the Agency's ingenuity and creativity, but the natural processes of government bureaucracy are also at work. Bureaucracies avoid risk, hate innovation, and seek to conceal their mistakes—and the CIA bureaucracy is no exception to the rule.

Reporters have a hard time confirming leaks out of CIA headquarters in Langley, Virginia, and newspapers therefore frequently do not press their reporters for corroboration of stories from intelligence sources. But because the CIA, like all intelligence organizations, deals in lies, it all too easily crosses the line between lying abroad to protect the nation and lying at home to protect itself—by, for example, blaming the Department of Defense or the Iraqi opposition for its own failures in Iraq. Sometimes CIA leaks are intended to show how clever the CIA is. Unfortunately, boastful descriptions of successful operations run the risk of making it more difficult to do the same thing, or something similar, again. By now every literate terrorist knows to avoid identifiable cell phones, not to buy airline tickets at the last minute, not to use ATMs, and the like.*

One final point: For many years, the CIA has made the recruitment of spies in target countries the basis for career ad-

---

* The FBI is at least as bad, maybe worse, in blabbing about its successes.

vancement. Recruit three Iranians and you are likely to move up faster than your colleague who can claim only one Egyptian. Bring in half a dozen of almost anything, and you are well on the way to a high-level position in the Directorate of Operations. These incentives encourage excessive zeal in recruiting, often to the annoyance of friendly countries where recruitment is easiest. They also tend to produce too many ill-informed or unreliable agents—and too many double agents.

Most troublingly, however, the heavy emphasis on agents causes the Agency to overemphasize the information delivered by those agents. And *that,* in turn, leads to an *under*emphasis on information that comes from other sources—such as, for example, noticing the obvious. Combine the emphasis on agent reports with a lack of language, historical, and cultural knowledge, and it suddenly becomes possible to understand how the CIA managed to miss a trend as large and sinister as the rise of extremist Islam.

A program of reform cannot stop with the intelligence services. It must also extend to our armed forces. The force we need for the future is substantially different from the force we field today.

The U.S. army bristles with tanks and howitzers. The navy is equipped to rush massive supplies of heavy equipment across the Atlantic Ocean. Our air force spends billions on fighters equipped to destroy sophisticated enemy combat jets—if, that is, any of our enemies have sophisticated combat jets to destroy.

These are forces of the past, built to counter threats that no longer exist. We must deal now with enemies who do not conduct military exercises that we can observe, who do not test weapons whose performance we can measure and anticipate, whose order of battle is constantly changing and largely unknown to us—and who may show up just about anywhere.

Will we need to go after a terrorist camp in some remote village in Indonesia? Or raid Syria to retrieve or destroy weapons of mass destruction that may have been sent there by Saddam Hussein for safekeeping? Or strike a decisive blow against a North Korean facility about to produce nuclear weapons for a terrorist customer? We face a daunting range of contingencies. To meet them, we must modernize the force left over from the cold war to make it far more flexible, far more agile, and far more cost-effective.

The ability actually to hit enemy targets is our first and most urgent priority. It is this more than anything else that distinguishes the future from the past. Ever since the first caveman put a rock in a sling, fighters have missed nearly every target they shot at. In the air campaign against Germany in World War II, only one bomb in four hundred struck *close to* its intended target. New technology enables us to transform the accuracy of forces, but the transition has not been easy and its completion will not be cheap.

We have made a start. During the Afghan campaign, an American reconnaissance aircraft spotted Taliban senior officials congregating at a house outside Kandahar. The aircraft fired a missile at the house, destroying it. The surviving Taliban raced to their trucks and sped off down the highway. The aircraft followed them, hurriedly signaling to a fighter jet on patrol nearby—which caught up with the caravan and wiped it out. All of this could have happened in any American war since 1917, with just one difference: The "pilot" of the reconnaissance plane was sitting the whole time at a console in Tampa, Florida. The aircraft was an unmanned reconnaissance drone called a Predator.

In Iraq, precision bombing left almost all the critical elements of Iraq's infrastructure intact: Bridges, dams, electricity, water, oil production and refining—all were spared in anticipation of the reconstruction that was sure to follow.* A visitor who walked through Baghdad in June would scarcely know that the city had been bombed in March. Politically as well as militarily, precision-strike airpower together with Special Forces is the decisive weapon in the war on terror—and our future conflicts as well. But we do not have enough of it, and what we do possess often lacks range. We need more unmanned aircraft and we need more highly accurate long-range bombers like the B-2. In the first eight weeks of the war over Kosovo, three B-2 aircraft, operating in weather conditions that kept much of the allied air force grounded, conducted 3 percent of the missions flown but destroyed 33 percent of the targets. Based on analysis of the Kosovo air campaign, two B-2 bombers can do the work of *seventy-eight* theater-based aircraft. And because they are nearly invisible to air defense radars, the enemy cannot easily shoot them down.

---

* We did destroy parts of the telecommunications system that were essential for Saddam's command and control.

The brilliant performance of our forces in Iraq hinted at what technology and a bold operational plan, superbly executed, can do. But much of the planning for, and debate about, the Iraq campaign exposed the grip of the dead hand of military tradition. A legion of retired generals took to the airwaves and went to Capitol Hill to say that we would need a substantially larger force in Iraq. And in the days when *they* commanded, that would have been true. But today's forces are vastly more efficient: Operation Iraqi Freedom showed the dramatic results of the first steps along the road of defense transformation. Much more remains to be done. Had the Pentagon been given its way in Iraq, it would have sent at least a quarter of a million soldiers to topple Saddam Hussein—the last of whom would not have arrived until midsummer of 2003, months after Baghdad fell to half as many troops.

The urgency of moving military forces to distant theaters quickly; the recognition that targets can often be destroyed more efficiently from the air than by ground forces; the realization that in modern war it is more important for ground forces to be *fast* than *big:* These ideas are about as welcome to some of the top brass as the abolition of horse cavalry was to their spiritual predecessors.

The cost of clinging to the past is *delay.* While the air campaign and the combined air-ground operations were the success story of Operation Iraqi Freedom, the painfully slow pace of the preparations for the operation was our largest problem. Thirteen months lapsed between President Bush's "axis of evil" speech and the arrival of American troops in

Baghdad on April 9, 2003. Tedious and frustrating though it was, diplomatic maneuvering at the United Nations cannot honestly be blamed for the long interval. The embarrassing truth is that we needed all those months to prepare and deploy our forces. Future enemies are unlikely to allow us to move so slowly.

At least the Department of Defense is led by people who understand the urgency of reform. Secretary of Defense Donald Rumsfeld played a central role in shaping the war plan for Iraqi Freedom, absorbed a fusillade of criticism during the few days when an army of second-guessers thought things were going badly, and then, when Baghdad fell, stood aside to credit our military forces with a brilliant victory. He has worked hard to encourage innovation, and he has been rewarded, as have other innovative leaders before him, with disparagement and opposition.*

At the Department of State, however, things continue pretty much as usual. State helped hasten out of the country every member of bin Laden's family and many other Saudi nationals. It fought tenaciously against requiring the same tourist visas from Saudi visitors that are required for other Middle Eastern nationals. It sought allies among "moderate" members of the Taliban and "moderate" members of the murderous Iranian regime. It pushed to broaden the CIA's

---

* "[Secretary Rumsfeld's] personal war against the U.S. Army is ending with a victory as complete as Saddam Hussein's defeat."—Robert Novak, "Don Rumsfeld's Army," May 1, 2003, available at www.townhall.com/columnists/robertnovak/rn20030501.shtml.

Syrian initiative into a full-fledged détente with the dictatorship in Damascus. It opposed the Iraq war to the end, and
then, after it lost that fight, battled to minimize the role of the
most democratically minded Iraqis in the postwar reconstruction of their country. There are exceptions, but as a
whole the department regards the war on terror with caution,
ambivalence, and sometimes open disparagement.

The Department of State conceives of its mission as promoting the best possible relationship between the United
States and other countries. For diplomats, diplomacy means
nurturing consensus. That usually means finding and enlarg-
ing those areas where the United States and foreign nations
can agree and glossing over those where we cannot. With
countries that share our values, principles, and interests,
these techniques of conciliation and accommodation achieve
good and useful results. But they are far from the appropriate
approaches to countries that wish to destroy us or that harbor groups with which we are at war.

The Department of State is charged with the task of representing the United States to the world. Most of its work is
done by the Foreign Service, a skilled, dedicated, and often
courageous professional fraternity. Foreign Service officers
are the civilian counterparts of the soldiers, sailors, airmen,
and marines of the Department of Defense, with one important difference: While our military invariably defers to the
policies of the commander in chief, the Foreign Service often
does not.

The most extreme example of this tendency is the now famous encounter between Saddam Hussein and April Glaspie, the career Foreign Service officer who headed our mission in Baghdad in 1990. At a meeting less than ninety-six hours before the invasion of Kuwait, Saddam Hussein dropped broad hints about his hostile plans. Glaspie responded with a disastrous green light: "We have no opinion on your Arab-Arab conflicts, such as your dispute with Kuwait." Glaspie's words have spawned a major conspiracy industry: Did the Bush administration secretly *want* Saddam to conquer Kuwait? Or was it perhaps luring the dictator to his destruction? Both scenarios are implausible. The United States had fought an undeclared naval war in the mid-1980s to protect Kuwait from Iran. What possible interest could we have in seeing Kuwait swallowed up by Iraq? As for the idea that Glaspie was cunningly goading Saddam, alas, that kind of imaginative scheming was the last thing to be expected from the elder George Bush's stodgy foreign-policy operation. This was the same George H. W. Bush who tried to *prevent the Soviet Union from disintegrating.* He refused to support the independence movements in the Baltic republics; he even traveled to Kiev in August 1991 to warn against the alleged perils of Ukrainian nationalism. This was not a presidency that invented clever snares for its enemies. Besides, if Glaspie's words were a trap, why did Bush then refuse to spring it? The Gulf War was halted as soon as the coalition had restored the status quo that prevailed on the day of Glaspie's fatal interview. We will never know whether the lives of a hundred Americans and of thousands of Kuwaitis and Iraqis—not to mention billions of dollars—might have been saved if only the U.S. ambassador had firmly told Saddam, "I wouldn't do that if I were you."

So what went wrong? The summer of 1990 was preoccupied with the enormous problem of German reunification and the future of Europe. At home, President Bush was engaged in intricate negotiations with Congress to reduce the federal budget deficit. He was not giving Iraq much thought. Whatever instructions Glaspie took into that room with the Iraqi dictator almost certainly emanated from the Department of State's Bureau of Near Eastern Affairs and were approved by White House staffers who saw the world much the way the bureau did, such as National Security Adviser Brent Scowcroft and his aide Richard Haass, now president of the Council on Foreign Relations. Glaspie's encounter with Saddam Hussein was not the first time that the Department of State maneuvered to achieve its own objectives rather than those of the president it nominally serves—and it would not be the last. When Undersecretary of State John Bolton made a bold speech on July 31, 2003, describing North Korea as a "hellish nightmare" in which Kim Jong Il "lived like royalty," a senior Foreign Service officer put it about that Bolton was speaking for himself; the president's own press secretary had to weigh in five days later to confirm that Bolton indeed spoke for the administration.

Here's how the department does its work. When the president adopts a policy or makes a statement that is anathema to the department, word goes out, usually by phone (cables

would leave tracks), instructing our diplomats abroad to report on the reaction of "their" governments. This sequence of
events then follows:

1. U.S. diplomats in foreign capitals find opposite numbers
   willing to say what their superiors back home want to
   hear.
2. The desired opinions are then fashioned into cables (as the
   department quaintly calls its communications) and sent
   back to Washington.
3. State Department officials express dismay at the poor re-
   ception the president's ideas or statements have elicited
   abroad.
4. State representatives begin drafting new policy papers to
   blunt, soften, or even scuttle the president's policy.
5. The policy that the president has already approved and articulated is then put up for debate all over again. It is rare
   that a new or modified policy does not result.

These are not new tactics. Richard Perle vividly recalls an
interagency meeting in the early days of the Reagan administration that was chaired by Assistant Secretary of State
Lawrence Eagleburger, an intelligent, witty, and wily Foreign
Service officer, who went on to serve as secretary of state in
the George H. W. Bush administration. The issue under discussion was a new arms control policy advocated by Perle,
who was then an assistant secretary of defense.

"The allies will never buy your policy," Eagleburger insisted. "If you put it forward, it will create unmanageable problems at NATO."

Perle responded: "But I've read all the incoming cables, and this issue doesn't get mentioned—not even a footnote." The meeting ended without a conclusion.

When the issue reappeared on the agenda two days later, Eagleburger walked into the meeting and threw a manila file on the table. "Here," he said, "are cables from London, Paris, Bonn, and NATO headquarters in Brussels. They came in yesterday. And they all warn against your policy."

Among all the departments of the United States government, the Department of State is the least ready to welcome into top policy positions the men and women chosen from outside by an elected president and confirmed by an elected Senate. From the point of view of the Foreign Service, every appointment at the level of assistant secretary or above that goes to an "outsider" is one less appointment available for a Foreign Service professional, and almost every such appointment triggers bruising battles between the White House personnel office and the department.

It is always unhealthy for a professional bureaucracy with deeply ingrained institutional biases to exclude outsiders and fresh thinking. But when the nation is challenged to move sharply in a new direction, and especially when a newly elected president sets out to change the course of American policy, such resistance can be actively subversive of representative government. Another Iraq example: In 1998, Congress wearied of the Clinton administration's inaction and enacted the Iraq Liberation Act, which authorized almost $100 million in aid for the Iraqi opposition to Saddam. The State Department and CIA lobbied furiously against spending the money and prevailed. Bill Clinton signed and praised the Iraq Liberation Act—and then eviscerated it. Even after George W. Bush replaced Clinton, the Iraq Liberation Act went largely unimplemented. How could this be? The White House makes foreign policy through the National Security Council—but a high proportion of the staff of the NSC is made up of State Department and CIA officers who spend a year or two, or sometimes longer, working for what ought to be the president's security policy staff. They import into the White House the dogmas and prejudices of their departments: Continuity of staff almost always means continuity of policy.

The caterwauling heard from the Department of State whenever a new thought is broached is also a product of the department's cumbersome organization. State is a jungle of cross-tabulated and contradictory bureaucracies. There is a bureau for each region of the world (Near East, Europe and Eurasia, Western Hemisphere, and so on), as well as a bureau for each major foreign policy issue or concern (international organizations, environment, human rights, refugees, and the like). As one would expect, there are frequent clashes among the regional bureaus, and then again between the regional bureaus and the "functional" bureaus, leading to endless meetings on thousands of issues, large and small. Frequently only the secretary of state (or his deputy) has the authority to settle these disputes, which frequently means that they do not get settled at all. One of the most common events in Washington is a high-level meeting at which there is one representative each from CIA, Defense, the FBI, and Homeland Security—and half a dozen from the State Department, who disagree with their State Department colleagues almost as fiercely as they do with all the other agencies.

Despite the absurd, often comical consequences of its byzantine bureaucracy, make no mistake: State is powerful. The State Department controls all official communications with other governments. This power is frequently abused: Hardly a day passes in which some message to which, say, the Department of Defense or Energy or Treasury objects is "inadvertently" dispatched without Defense or Energy or Treasury reading it. Not so often, but often enough, cables that have been adopted over State's objections are "inadvertently" forgotten. State even controls the travel overseas of officials from other government departments. One favorite trick: If a State Department bureau gets wind that an official from another department may say or do something with which it disagrees on a mission abroad, it will simply deny that official "country clearance," thus preventing him or her from traveling.

All of this would be troubling enough in normal times. But these are not normal times. We are at war. The determination of the State Department to reconcile the irreconcilable, to negotiate the unnegotiable, and to appease the unappeasable is an obstacle to victory.

There are dozens of changes that need to be made to our institutions so that they can put a bold antiterrorism strategy into effect. These are the four most urgent:

Reform the FBI

THE FBI MUST return to the job it does best: catching criminals. It should be fired from the counterterrorism job it has bungled, and its counterterrorism units and employees should be reassigned to a new domestic intelligence agency.

This new domestic intelligence agency should report not to the attorney general, but to the secretary of homeland security. The agency's mission would be founded on the insight that terrorist noncitizen suspects are not alleged criminals entitled to the protections that Americans grant their fellow citizens accused of breaking the law. Noncitizen terrorist suspects are not members of the American national community, and they have no proper claim on the rights Americans accord one another. They are suspected of being enemy *combatants,* as hostile and merciless as the assassins of the SS or KGB, but, unlike them, eager to accept a martyr's fate. We should care less about prosecuting and punishing them than about squeezing information out of them about their organization and their associates. The Immigration and Naturalization Service already has the power to hold and question illegal aliens suspected of terrorist involvement and the right to use evidence acquired from intelligence sources rather than through the full process of American criminal law. That the

INS has proven itself incompetent in these matters reinforces the case for starting fresh with a new domestic intelligence organization.

Reform the CIA

THE CIA REQUIRES reform as much as the FBI, but it presents a much tougher challenge. The problem starts at the very top: Put the CIA in the hands of a brilliant visionary like William Casey and leave him in office long enough to overhaul the place and you get one kind of CIA. Turn it over to Jimmy Carter's Stansfield Turner and you get quite another. George Tenet has been the director of central intelligence since 1997, time enough to have changed the Agency's culture. He has failed. He should go.

The CIA in 2004 remains to a disturbing degree the same bureaucratic, nervous, and often highly politicized institution it was during the Clinton years. Individual successes—and, to be fair, there have been some—are not enough. The CIA must be renovated from top to bottom by leaders who think less about the wishes of the CIA bureaucracy and more the security needs of the American people.

The clandestine service ended up inside the CIA back in the 1940s largely by accident, and it has not always been a happy accident. The job the Special Forces did in Afghanistan (organizing and directing the Taliban's domestic enemies) is not easy to distinguish from the job the CIA did (finding and bribing the Taliban's domestic enemies). Indeed, a high percentage of the CIA personnel involved in paramilitary operations have been recruited directly out of the U.S. military. During the Afghanistan campaign, one Defense Department official said, "I keep hearing about the great performance of the CIA in Afghanistan. But those are *our* guys on *their* payroll." It may be time to bring all of these secret warriors into a single paramilitary structure ultimately answerable to the secretary of defense, the man responsible for running America's wars, both those fought in the open and those that must be waged in the shadows.

Removing operations from CIA control would focus the attention of the CIA's leadership on their core mission: information-gathering. The CIA must reemphasize linguistic competence—and must overcome its reluctance to check, double-check, and triple-check the loyalties of native-born speakers of the languages in which we are most interested. Since 2001, there have been three publicized cases of alleged serious sabotage or treachery in the armed forces, with more apparently still under investigation as this book goes to press.* There have been rumors of similar cases in the security services, where such betrayals could potentially carry even more fatal consequences.

---

* Sergeant Hasan Karim Akbar of the 101st Airborne Division is alleged to have attacked his fellow soldiers with hand grenades at a camp in Kuwait in March 2003, killing one and wounding fifteen. Captain James Yee, a chaplain at Guantánamo, was charged with spying and aiding the enemy in September 2003. Senior Airman Ahmad I. al-Halabi, a translator at Guantánamo, was also charged with espionage and passing military secrets in September 2003; he may have belonged to the same ring as Yee. *The New York Times* reported on September 24, 2003, that other Guantánamo personnel are also under investigation.

Domestic intelligence-gathering should continue to be segregated from foreign spying, both for civil liberties reasons and to ensure that the president and national leaders have access to more than one source of information. For this reason too, the CIA's long-standing ambition to grab control of the Defense Intelligence Agency and the National Security Agency should be beaten back. In intelligence as in medicine, there is no substitute for a second opinion.

Reform the Pentagon

BETWEEN 1990 AND 2000, we cut defense spending as a share of our economy by almost one-third, from 4.8 percent to barely 3 percent. These drastic cuts in defense (along with the "new economy" technology boom of the 1990s) allowed the Clinton administration to increase social welfare spending rapidly while also reducing national budget deficits. Now the defense budget is rising again—but nowhere near as far or as fast as it fell. By the time the Bush defense increases all arrive, we'll still be spending only about two-thirds as much of our income on defense as we did in the mid-1980s. There will not be a lot of loose defense cash to spare. We cannot afford to squander a nickel of it.

Every dollar that goes to keeping open a redundant base or obsolete maintenance facility is a dollar that cannot be spent to make our troops safer or more effective.

The army, navy, and air force split the defense budget into three roughly equal portions, year after year. It is unlikely that this amazing coincidence is the product of careful analysis.

We should invest in battlefield productivity in exactly the same way that private industry invests in productivity in the factory and office. No operational commander should have to assign a soldier to a task that could be done as well by a computer, a remote sensor, or an unmanned airplane. Our troops are the best in the world. They stand ready to make the ultimate sacrifice for their country. They should not be asked to do things that can be done more effectively *and with less risk* by capital equipment. But today there is no practical mechanism for deciding, for example, that we could get by with ten fewer soldiers who cost $65,000 per year per person by substituting a $650,000-a-year expenditure on automated perimeter surveillance systems. The armed forces need to do what private industry does: scrupulously study their operations to find where and how equipment can be substituted for people, in every operation from close combat to managing motor pools.

Reform the State Department

TO STIFFEN STATE'S spine, we should abolish, or at the very least downgrade, the regional bureaus: Near Eastern Affairs, Western Hemisphere Affairs, and all the rest. The people at, say, the Guatemala desk are already reporting to a dozen bureaus covering the major topics of U.S. interest, from trade to human rights. Eliminating the regional bureaus would streamline the State Department's ponderous bureaucracy—and protect State from its tendency to forget that it is working for the *American* people. Staff at the refugee bureau or the environmental bureau have relatively clear missions. The people at Near Eastern Affairs or Western Hemisphere Affairs do not. As a result, they tend over time to invent their own missions, and the most obvious available mission is to become the bureaucratic champions of the wishes and desires of the governments in their area of responsibility. They stop representing America to the world and begin representing the world to America.

Next, we should increase sharply the number of political appointees in the State Department and expand their role. The prejudice against political appointees in our diplomatic service is really a prejudice against democratic oversight of our foreign policy. We need ambassadors who will forcefully and unapologetically champion American policy abroad, and since our policies are set by the president, they will be most vigorously articulated by appointees who understand the president's mind and are sympathetic to his policies. The press delights in repeating horror stories about political ambassadors. But we are unaware of any amateur diplomat ever making a mistake as disastrous as that made by the consummately professional Glaspie. In the Middle East especially, our foreign policies have deviated from the moral principles and common sense of the American people. The policies need to be yanked back into line. The individuals most likely to yank them back successfully are individuals who share those principles and that sense.

Back at Foggy Bottom, all the *policy-making*, as opposed to *policy-implementing*, jobs should rotate with each change of administration to people who broadly support the goals and policies of that administration. People who do not support the president's policies should not have a hand in making them.

Oh—and it might also be time to upgrade State's counter-terrorism chief from a mere ambassador-at-large, the same rank as the chief protocol officer, to a full-fledged undersecretary with a bureau of his own behind him.

BEHIND ALL THESE institutional reforms, we need a reform of the spirit. In the little more than two years since 9/11—the same space of time in which our grandparents swept from disaster and humiliation at Pearl Harbor to triumph at Guadalcanal and in Sicily—many of our leaders have succumbed to a troubling weakening of the spirit, a disturbing lapse of grit and seriousness. In a speech at New York University in August 2003, former vice president Gore made the stunning assertion that the United States government under George Bush has ceased to be one that "upholds the fundamental rights even of those it believes to be its captured enemies." Even in the midst of a global struggle, this prominent American apparently cannot free himself from the delusion that foreign terrorists are to be read their *Miranda* rights before they are questioned.

The United States is proud to call itself a nation ruled by law. But even a nation of laws must understand the limits of legalism. Between 1861 and 1865, the government of the United States took tens of thousands of American citizens prisoner and detained them for years without letting any one of them see a lawyer. We targeted and shot down the plane of the Japanese admiral who had planned Pearl Harbor and felt not a twinge of remorse at his extrajudicial killing. War has its rules, of course—but by those very rules our enemies in this war on terror are outlaws.

Above all, we need to reanimate the nation's innate optimism about the outcome of this fight. We have an immense battle ahead of us. But so do the terrorists. In the pre-9/11 world in which their acts of terror went unrequited, their ambitions soared. But by now they have begun to face three realities: Terrorism costs money—lots of it; terrorism is difficult; and terrorism requires state support. These realities do not favor the terrorists—and with the right strategy and tactics we can make them even more unfavorable.

After 9/11, there was a lot of loose talk about how the World Trade Center attacks had cost less than $100,000. That makes as much sense as computing the cost of the shoot-out that killed Uday and Qusay Hussein by tallying the price of the bullets fired. The true cost of 9/11 includes the cost of recruiting and training the hundreds of jihad fighters from whom al-Qaeda selected the carefully chosen nineteen. It includes the cost of operating the camps in which the terrorists were trained. It includes, too, the cost of buying the support first of the Sudan government and then of the Afghan Taliban. And it includes, finally, the whole infrastructure of extremist Islam that created the terror networks in the first place. An accurate accounting of the cost of 9/11 would sound like one of those credit card commercials on television: "Plane fares, box cutters, petty cash: $100,000. Recruiting, training, and protecting thousands of suicide bombers: millions. Acquiring ideological and territorial bases of your own: priceless."

If we can squeeze or cut off the terrorists' money, we can dramatically reduce their ability to strike.

Terrorism costs money because terrorism is *difficult*—and this is another reality. It requires capable agents and sophisticated planning, and every stage along the way is fraught with danger: Identifying potential agents is difficult, recruiting them is difficult, training them is difficult, and preventing counterterrorism agencies from infiltrating along with those new recruits is even more difficult. Slipping them past the police and immigration authorities of the United States and other countries is not as difficult as it should be, but it is getting more so. Devising workable terrorist operations is always difficult, and so is communicating those plans to everyone who needs to know them and keeping them secret from everyone who does not.

Imagine for a moment being an al-Qaeda operative in the United States today. You are likely to be alone and isolated, surrounded by a population that is looking for you and ready to turn you in to the police. You have to worry whether the mosques you frequent are watched by the FBI—and whether the Arabic-speaking landlord who rents you a room is not perhaps an informer. After 9/11, Americans were shocked to learn how close the authorities came to catching the plotters before they struck. From the point of view of the terrorists, however, the revelations suggest a very different moral: If the police nearly caught the terrorists in the lax days before 9/11, what would be a terror team's chances *today*?

Because terrorism is already so difficult, the terrorists may already be near their tipping point—the point at which even their supporters will perceive that terrorism is not only pointless but actually counterproductive. We may need only to make terrorism marginally more difficult to push the terrorists past that tipping point to paralysis.

A third reality is that because terrorism is difficult, terrorists almost always require some kind of support from a government somewhere. Genuinely independent terror groups have seldom managed to survive very long: Think of the Weather Underground in the United States back in the late 1960s, or Armenian and Croatian terrorism in the 1980s, or Timothy McVeigh's pointless militia movement. These organizations inflicted grief and suffering in their time, but they achieved nothing for the causes they espoused, and they were all apprehended and crushed in fairly short order. Effective terrorists either are backed by governments (as Iraq backed Abu Nidal, as Iran backs Hezbollah) or else they create territorial bases for themselves in which they practically *become* the government, as the Revolutionary Armed Forces of Colombia have done—and as al-Qaeda did in Afghanistan. Indeed, of the most murderous attacks on America or Americans in the two decades before 9/11, only Timothy McVeigh's was *not* directed or supported by a foreign state.*

The linkage between terror groups and terror states has become even more intimate as both terrorists and terror states seek and acquire weapons of mass destruction: nerve agents and other lethal chemical agents, anthrax and other biological agents, radioactive materials, and—the ultimate prize—nuclear weapons. Weapons of mass destruction are critical to modern terrorism in two ways: First, and most obviously, they can be used directly as instruments of murder. In 1994 and 1995, the Japanese terror group Aum Shinrikyo used sarin gas to murder nineteen people and injure thousands more in two attacks, one on the town of Matsumoto and then in the Tokyo subway system. The anthrax killers of October 2002 murdered five people with poison sent through the mails. Exploding radioactive material in an American town could kill thousands and render large areas uninhabitable for years. As for nuclear bombs—well, their potential is obvious. Indeed, Islamic terror groups now have almost no choice but to try to acquire weapons of mass destruction. The terror attacks of 9/11 raised the bar for politically effective terror: If al-Qaeda's next operation on U.S. soil were to kill, say, fourteen people, al-Qaeda's supporters in the Muslim world would almost certainly conclude that the group had

---

* At least, so far as we know. On the other hand, our American Enterprise Institute colleague Laurie Mylroie has developed evidence not yet conclusive that links McVeigh to telephone numbers in the Philippines that are known to have been used by terrorists.

been fatally weakened. To prove its continuing power, al-Qaeda must plot attacks at least as destructive as those of 9/11—and weapons of mass destruction are probably the only means with which it can achieve that end.

Second and less obvious, but in the long run probably more important, is the *strategic* value of weapons of mass destruction to terrorists and their backers. Terror-sponsoring governments always have to worry that if they leave their fingerprints behind on an attack, their victims will retaliate—as the United States did when Libyan agents blew up a West Berlin nightclub in 1986, killing two U.S. servicemen and one civilian and wounding two hundred others. And since the governments that sponsor terror are ultimately weaker than those they victimize, retaliation is a significant danger for them. Nuclear weapons are the great equalizer: They can deter retaliation by even the most powerful and outraged governments. In December 2001, a Kashmiri terrorist group that had at various times been supported by the Pakistani intelligence services carried out a gun and grenade attack on the Indian parliament in New Delhi. The Kashmiri terrorists killed five policemen and a gardener; one of the policemen died saving the life of India's vice president, Krishan Kant. India blamed Pakistan and mobilized its army. The Pakistanis were unapologetic, and war might well have broken out had the Indians not been deterred by Pakistan's nuclear force. In the end, India settled for a quiet promise from Pakistan to rein in the Kashmiri groups. (It should be said that as of the fall of 2003, the promise has been honored.)

This reality implies that we can drastically curtail terrorism by destroying those regimes that offer terrorists safe harbor—and by acting decisively to prevent regimes with terror connections from acquiring weapons of mass destruction.

Here's a fourth and final reality: It's easier to recruit potential terrorists when the terror group seems to be winning than when it is losing. The left-wing terrorist groups that attempted to destabilize Western Europe in the 1970s went out of business in the 1980s. Why? In 1977 and 1978, the groups seemed radical, daring, and effective—the Italian Red Brigades succeeded in kidnapping and murdering a former prime minister; the German Red Army Faction did the same to the head of the German employers' association. Chic philosophers like Michel Foucault endorsed the terrorists' crimes, and they were portrayed sympathetically in movies like the 1980 German film *Knife in the Head*. But the voters of Western Europe hung tough and elected conservative leaders like Helmut Kohl and Margaret Thatcher. The leaders of the Red Brigades and the Red Army Faction were caught and jailed. Their sponsor, the Soviet Union, disintegrated—and before long left-wing European terrorism had vanished. Nobody wants to die on a fool's errand.

Terrorists, in other words, are motivated by ideology. Discredit the ideology and you defeat the terrorists.

In all the long years in which we suffered terrorist attacks and did not hit back, it was never because we were too weak to respond. It was always a matter of imagination and of will. It still is.

8. FRIENDS AND FOES

THE 1990S WERE a decade of illusions in foreign policy. On September 11, 2001, this age of illusion ended. The United States asked its friends and allies to join in the fight against terror—and discovered that after the first emotional expressions of sympathy for the victims, those friends and allies were prepared to do little. September 11 revealed what Americans had been concealing from themselves for far too long: The end of the cold war and the emergence of the United States as the world's superpower had not put an end to the rivalries and animosities of nations. It had simply redirected them—often against the United States.

Soldiers warn that when you draw up a plan, you must always remember that the enemy gets a vote on whether it can be put into effect. The same is true for your friends, and especially your fair-weather friends. So as we draw up our plans for the war on terror, we must bear in mind what our friends as well as our enemies are doing and thinking, not merely what they find it convenient to say to us and to others.

The jealousy and resentment that animate the terrorists also affect many of our former cold war allies. The French call the United States a "hyperpower." We are, they say, simultaneously the strongest military, economic, and cultural force on the planet—as France was 250 years ago. Unsurprisingly, they are not overjoyed by our good fortune.

Obviously, we are a country blessed with good friends all around the world. Even people who want to hate the United States are often seduced by the allure of American culture. Jacques Chirac often tells the story of how he came to the United States to study at Harvard—and how he learned even more from his weekend job serving sodas at a Howard Johnson's off campus. In 1953, it would simply have been inconceivable for a young Frenchman from a good family to take a job in France as a waiter; it was in the United States that Jacques Chirac got his first glimpse of social equality. He was not the first—nor will he be the last—European to be reinvigorated in his democratic ideals by the American example.

So while our friendships are real, the dream of the early 1990s was not. Too many Americans took the first Gulf War as a model for our future security. In 1990, President George H. W. Bush assembled a global coalition that spanned the United States, Europe, Russia, China, and many Arab countries and even got a UN Security Council authorizing force. A rogue aggressor was struck down by the wrath of a united world. It had never happened before; it would have been highly unrealistic to expect such a thing ever to happen again.

Yet through the 1990s, we seemed to believe that a "new world order" had fallen into place. The idea took hold in the United States, and in many other Western countries, that the anomalous war in the Gulf had set the standard for all future military conflicts. Whenever a crisis erupted over the next ten years—in Haiti, in Rwanda, in Bosnia, in Kosovo—the Clinton administration would seek to assemble another grand coalition that could gain the blessing of the United Nations. In the minds of many, Kofi Annan's Secretariat replaced the United States Congress as the body entitled to decide whether and when the United States was permitted to wage war.

Each and every one of these excursions in multilateralism ended in disappointment—or worse.

There was actually a UN force present in Rwanda when the massacres erupted there in 1994. It barricaded itself away and allowed the killings to proceed uninterrupted.

In the former Yugoslavia, the UN instituted a system of sanctions that denied arms equally to the already well-armed Serbians and to the entirely disarmed Bosnian Muslims. The effect was entirely predictable: Bosnian Muslims were left hopelessly vulnerable to well-armed thugs, whose forces slaughtered men, women, and children, sometimes within sight of United Nations "peacekeepers" sent to protect them. Russia used its Security Council veto to frustrate UN-sanctioned military operations against Serbia. When, at length, the NATO alliance took up the fight against Serbia in Kosovo, a French officer at NATO headquarters in Brussels was caught leaking bombing targets to the Serbian military.*

In Iraq, the record is more pitiful still: The UN would pass resolutions, France and Russia would block enforcement, and then Kofi Annan would jet to Baghdad to negotiate with the dictator which of the UN's solemn resolutions would apply and which would not.

We can afford illusions no longer. We have a big mission ahead of us. Let us ready ourselves for the task by examining with clear eyes the roster of our supporters and our opponents, open and disguised.

Europe

AMERICANS HAVE BEEN disappointed and often angered during the war on terror to discover that many of our most important democratic allies have distanced themselves from our struggle—or even opposed important elements of our

---

* The officer was Major Pierre-Henri Bunel, chief of staff to France's permanent representative on the NATO military committee in Brussels. Bunel was charged with and convicted of treason to France and sentenced to five years' imprisonment. However, suspicions linger in other NATO countries that Bunel's leak was authorized by his superiors, and for four reasons: 1) Bunel was arrested by the French only after his activities were detected by a non-French secret service. 2) Bunel had received no money or other compensation from the Serbians, ruling out the usual motive for espionage. 3) When caught, Bunel had originally insisted that his motive was humanitarian; when later, to his apparent surprise, he found himself on trial, he insisted loudly that he had been following orders. 4) Finally and most suggestive, other French officers appear to have leaked military information to Serb leaders during the Bosnian conflict. France had strongly backed the Serbians up until 1995, and many in NATO suspected that the French government never sincerely altered its view afterward.

strategy. For half a century, Americans risked nuclear annihilation to defend the continent of Europe against Soviet aggression. Instead, by a twist of fate, the first foreign assault against a NATO country landed on American soil—and Americans turned about to discover what the allies for whom Americans had been prepared to die were, in their turn, prepared to do for Americans. The disconcerting answer was: Not much. It is true that NATO secretary-general George Robertson asked for and got a declaration from NATO invoking Article V of the NATO Charter, the famous pledge that "an attack against one is an attack against all." And some NATO allies—including Italy, Spain, Poland, Portugal, and little Denmark—and other friends of the United States have gone out of their way to be helpful.

But even during the campaign in Afghanistan, which was supported unanimously by all the NATO governments, the United States encountered a surprising truculence on the part of allied governments over seemingly minor issues. France, for example, refused to provide information about the case of Zacarias Moussaoui, the alleged twentieth 9/11 hijacker, if U.S. prosecutors demanded the death penalty for him. Even more disheartening was the unconcealed hostility of much of the European press, which credulously reprinted (among other lies) the charge that the United States "tortured" al-Qaeda captives by handcuffing them and giving them earplugs for the long and noisy flight in a military transport from Afghanistan to Guantánamo Bay. The hostile drumbeat of the European press had its effect on public opinion: French book buyers grabbed three hundred thousand copies of a book that claimed the 9/11 attacks were a hoax orchestrated by the Pentagon. (A similar book, this one by a former German cabinet minister, climbed the charts in Germany in 2003.)

Things tumbled further downhill in 2002. A disturbing number of our NATO allies took the view that we should have declared victory and gone home after routing the Taliban. As far as these halfhearted allies were concerned, once al-Qaeda was driven out of Afghanistan, the war on terror became a mere police matter. They refused to join us in pressuring Iraq, Iran, or North Korea. They showed an astonishing lack of curiosity about the terror links of Saudi Arabia and the other Arab states. Indeed, if we had listened to the Europeans, the only Middle Eastern regime we would have singled out for political pressure in 2002 would have been *Israel*.

To Americans, this looked like appeasement. But it would be a great mistake to attribute European appeasement to cowardice—or to cowardice alone. The same European governments that hesitated to confront terrorists were more than prepared to oppose *us*. In the weeks leading up to the Iraq campaign, French president Jacques Chirac volunteered as Saddam Hussein's most important ally and protector. Chirac's warm reminiscences about his youthful experiences in the United States contrast sharply with the open hostility of his government to U.S. policy in the war on terror. That is what it is—and it is foolish to pretend otherwise. French foreign minister Dominique de Villepin jetted around Africa, offering bribes to France's former colonies to vote against the United States at the UN on the second Iraq resolution. Chirac actually threatened to bar the new democracies of central Europe from the European Union if they joined the U.S.-led coalition against Iraq. When the leaders of some of those democracies signed an open letter supporting the United States, Chirac scolded them for having "missed a good opportunity to shut up." Then France went over the top: In February 2003, it led the opposition within NATO to dispatching air defense units to protect Turkey, a NATO member, if Iraq attacked it—a shocking break with the long history and essential purpose of the NATO alliance.

And as they gleefully smashed up an alliance that had kept the peace of the world for half a century, the ministers of the Chirac government preened and congratulated themselves. "The president of France and the pope"—in that order—"saved the world from a 'clash of civilizations,' " a high French official told a conference in Europe in the spring of 2003.

And where France led, other NATO countries followed: Germany most importantly, but also France's pilot fish, Belgium. Outside NATO, France's anti-American campaign had a damaging effect as well, emboldening Russia to adopt an anti-American stance that it would not have dared adopt on its own.

Everyone can understand that allies sometimes disagree. The United States has never demanded unthinking obedience from its friends. In the case of Iraq, the United States clearly and repeatedly declared that we were not asking our allies to do anything with which they were not comfortable. There was no pressure, no demand that others join in sending troops or that they provide any other form of assistance. We *did* expect that we would not be denied permission to fly over allied territory in reaching targets in Afghanistan and Iraq, but that was certainly not asking for much. Mostly we asked simply that those of our friends who disagreed with us refrain from actively opposing our military operations. The enthusiasm and persistence with which France, Germany, and some others set themselves to obstruct and thwart American policy: This was something new and deeply troubling.

A certain sort of behavior defines a healthy relationship among friends and allies: a readiness to grant the benefit of the doubt where a credible claim of a vital national interest is put forward. Thus, President Reagan took immediate action to support our British allies when Argentina invaded the Falkland Islands in 1982, even though that support had the potential to damage our interests in Latin America. But perhaps the story that best illustrates how friends should treat friends involves, ironically, France—but the France of a different era. When the United States caught the Soviet Union shipping ballistic missiles to Castro's Cuba in 1962, President Kennedy ordered our top-secret satellite photographs to be shown to our closest allies in advance of Adlai Stevenson's famous presentation to the UN Security Council. Former secretary of state Dean Acheson was dispatched to Paris to brief President de Gaulle. Before Acheson could begin, de Gaulle waved the pictures away. He told Acheson that he did not need to see any photographs. If the president of the United States said he had reason to act, that was good enough for de Gaulle. And he then promised France's full support. Now, to be sure, President Chirac is no de Gaulle, and relations between the United States and France are not what they were in 1962. But whoever thought the day would come when a French foreign minister would refuse to answer the question "Whom do you want to win?" about a war an ally would soon fight?

The president's critics in Europe (and even some in this country) have attributed French and German noncooperation, at least in part, to the resentment in those countries of Bush's "unilateralism." But what some Europeans decry as "unilateralism" many Americans regard as *leadership*. The concept of leadership implies a willingness to act in a good cause, even—indeed, especially—when others are reluctant to do so. First Bosnia and then Kosovo should remind us that when the United States recoiled temporarily from leadership, Europe, for all its brave talk, would not act to defend what Europeans themselves regarded as their highest values and most precious interests.

Many Europeans will concede all this. They will say that they are not questioning America's leadership, but that they are offended by President Bush's refusal to embrace policies that European opinion supports: the Kyoto accord on global warming, for example, or the International Criminal Court (ICC).

We can understand why the American position on these issues rankles. The United States is so big and so important that when it refuses to sign up for Kyoto or the ICC, it effectively wrecks the whole agreement—a de facto American veto. Nobody likes to be reminded that some other country matters more in the world than his own.

But with both Kyoto and the ICC, President Bush inherited an untenable situation from his feckless predecessor. It had been obvious for many years that neither agreement had the faintest hope of passing the Senate, even when the Senate was controlled by Democrats. The Senate actually put itself on record 95–0 against Kyoto. But President Clinton could never bring himself to take decisive action. He flinched from asking the Europeans to renegotiate the treaties to make them more acceptable to American opinion: That would have offended his environmentalist supporters. He flinched from submitting the treaties to the Senate and arguing for them as best he could: That would have been too risky politically. Nor would he candidly acknowledge to the Europeans that the United States would not ratify: That would have been too painful after all those years of negotiating. So instead he kept stringing the Europeans along, promiscuously promising them that he would conjure up the votes somehow. In the case of Kyoto, which the United States signed on December 11, 1997, Clinton strung the Europeans along for more than *three years* before Bush delivered the bad news that the agreement would never pass the U.S. Senate.

But can it really be "unilateral" for the United States to

hold a different view of an international treaty from that of our European allies? Surely nations are free to decide which treaty commitments they will accept and which they will reject. If that is unilateralism, then we are all unilateralists.

If it is true that some of our traditional allies tried to undermine our Iraq policy because of resentment over other policy differences, we have every reason to be deeply aggrieved. After all, the Europeans frequently do things we don't like, but we would never consider that grounds for refusing to come to their aid in time of war. Can you imagine President Reagan shrugging off the security of Germany or France back in the 1980s to protest their farm subsidies?

The 1980s were no golden age. Anti-American antagonisms flourished in Europe then, too. But those antagonisms were for the most part suppressed. Without the United States, Europe could not defend itself against the massive military power of the Soviet Union, and Europeans knew it. But now the Soviet Union no longer menaces Western Europe, and American power is no longer perceived as essential to Europe's survival. Now long-pent-up misgivings about American policies and power are free to rise—to *gush*—to the surface. A flood of resentment has inundated the continent.

"Why does he hate me so much? I never did anything for him." It's an old Hollywood joke, but it has wide applicability. The United States spent hundreds of billions over half a century doing things for Europe, and, inevitably, many Europeans resent it. They resent America's ability to be generous, and they resent their need for that generosity. For such people, the collapse of the Soviet Union was a moment of liberation—not for the Eastern Europeans whom the Soviets had enslaved, but for *themselves*. Now at last they could be free of the United States and of the horrible burden of gratitude. And it's probably not coincidence that the countries in Europe where anti-Americanism runs strongest are those that have the most reason to feel grateful: France, which the United States liberated; and Germany, which the United States reconstructed and protected.

Absent the Soviet Union, many Europeans are deciding that the American power that used to defend them has in the span of just a few years become a threat. The French Foreign Ministry, the Brussels bureaucracy, and even some British officials now talk openly about building a European superpower that can act as a "counterweight" against the United States. "France cannot accept a unipolar world or the unilateralism of a single hyperpower," former French foreign minister Hubert Vedrine intoned in 1998. Indeed, one important motivation of "globalist" projects like Kyoto and the ICC has been to entangle the United States in restrictions that restrain its power until the new Europe can challenge it.

The birth of this new Europe was announced prematurely in 1991, when Jacques Poos, then foreign minister of Luxembourg, urged the United States to butt out of the Yugoslavian crisis: "This is the hour of Europe, not the hour of the Americans." Poos's timing was premature, but his thinking was prophetic. Through the 1990s, the governments of Europe toiled to create a new European political system that could use the continent's wealth to create a European superpower, independent of—and quietly hostile to—the United States.

The United States has long supported European unification. A united Europe, American policy makers believed, would have a stronger economy and could better contribute to the common defense against the Soviet Union. American business approved of the idea, too: From Lisbon to Hamburg is only as far as from New York to Houston, but a truck making the journey can cross up to six international borders. For corporations used to the vast internal market of the United States, a European Union seemed the plainest common sense.

The possibility that the integrated Europe we had nurtured for so long might emerge as a "counterweight" to the United States, particularly on the most sensitive issues of national security, would never have occurred to the Eurocentric American foreign policy establishment. And now that it is happening, they still find it almost impossible to believe their eyes.

So what should we do? These four things.

First, acknowledge that a more closely integrated Europe is no longer an unqualified American interest. Yes, this is an abrupt change from the past. But as John Maynard Keynes quipped to a critic who accused him of changing his mind, "When the facts change, I change my opinions. What do you do, sir?"

Second, we should start a debate within Europe over the French ambition to build the European Union into an anti-American counterweight. The European Union will soon comprise twenty-six nations. Many of them, probably a large majority of them, strongly disapprove of the French vision for Europe. We should support these European friends: Isolated, or allied only with Belgium and Luxembourg, France would have little prospect of building Europe in opposition to the United States. (We are optimistic that once Chancellor Gerhard Schroeder leaves the scene, Germany will revert to its accustomed friendliness. Indeed, Foreign Minister Fischer has already begun to signal Germany's discomfort with the French "counterweight" idea. In a speech in May 2003, he said, "Not a single problem in the world can be solved if Europe, Canada and the United States are at odds."*)

Third, France may well persist in its counterweight strategy despite our best efforts to organize opposition within Europe. Such persistence should be attended with costs. Indeed, we can hardly expect other Europeans to oppose French policy if *we* take no action to do so. While the deterioration of the French-American relationship is damaging to both France and the United States, it would be far worse for us to become passive victims of a hostile French diplomacy, as in the case of Iraq, or to acquiesce in the transformation of the European Union into an unfriendly power. We should remain ready for the fullest cooperation with France on political, military, intelligence, trade, and other matters. But we should calibrate the nature and extent of that cooperation to reflect French behavior. For now, this might well mean canceling or scaling

---

* www.auswaertiges-amt.de/www/en/ausgabe_archiv?archiv_id=4565.

back cooperative defense and intelligence programs and downgrading the political relationship. Here are some concrete suggestions:

- In 1995, newly elected French president Jacques Chirac promised to lead France back into NATO's integrated military command, which France had quit in 1967. The promise was never honored. Today, France claims to be a member in full standing of NATO, even as it fails to contribute to the alliance's essential purposes. We should insist that all-important NATO business be conducted by NATO's military council, on which France does not sit. And we can *visibly* limit our cooperation with France's military and intelligence services to reflect the level of political cooperation we receive from France. We must put an end to the double game whereby France helps itself to all the benefits of alliance while shrugging off the alliance's obligations.

- We can conduct elements of our political and economic relationship with the European Union in a manner that drives home the price all of Europe pays when it accepts parochial, self-interested French policies. Europe's ultra-protectionist agricultural policy is a good example; so is opposition to genetically modified foods; so, finally, is France's policy of squandering scarce defense resources on expensive and ineffective weapons whose only merit is that they are made in France.

- We should force European governments to choose between Paris and Washington. Naturally, *they* would rather not

confront such a choice. But why is it in *our* interest to help
them wriggle out of it? Most European governments attach
a lot more importance to the transatlantic relationship than
they do to grand French fancies like a European defense
union. The French sidle past that problem by assuring the
other European governments that they can belong to both.
We need to make sure they understand that they cannot.

- We ought to actively support the enlargement of the EU and
  of NATO. The bigger the EU grows, the less amenable it
  will become to French aspirations to boss the other states.
  Better still, the new democracies of central and Eastern Europe attach great importance to their relationship with the
  United States. From Riga to Sofia, young people are studying English, not French, and hoping for jobs with Microsoft
  and Citibank, not some nationalized French bureaucracy.
  Above all, countries that only recently escaped from Soviet
  domination (and that remain anxious about Russia's future
  intentions) will for many years prefer the hard certainty
  of an American military alliance to the easy, inflationary
  currency offered by Paris. "One lesson from the 1930s,"
  quipped an unnamed but very senior Czech official when
  asked to explain his country's keenness to enter NATO:
  "No more French security guarantees."

Dealing with France is important, but the fourth thing we
need to do to enhance our strategic position in Europe is the
most important of all: We must do our utmost to preserve our
British ally's strategic independence *from* Europe.

Americans appreciated Britain's support in Afghanistan and Iraq, but we were not surprised by it—after all, the two countries have been joined in a uniquely intimate defense partnership since 1941. Yet had the 9/11 attacks occurred half a dozen years later, it is entirely possible that Britain could not have supported us at all. Britain in 2001 was well along the way to submitting itself to a common European foreign policy and to committing its armed forces, the most capable in Europe, to a European rapid reaction force. Had those policies been consummated, Blair's successor might well have had little more to offer us when we asked for his help than sincere sympathy and best wishes. He might well have been bound to follow the policy laid down by the French, Germans, Belgians, and others, and his most deployable soldiers might well have been integrated into a military unit from which extraction would be neither easy nor quick.

This is a future we should resist. Of course, Americans recognize the importance to Britain of its economic links with the continent of Europe. Americans also understand why Britain would want a voice in the governance of the European Union. But that system of governance is a trap: a one-way ticket into an "ever closer" union that aspires to transform Europe into a single state with a single currency, a single president, a single constitution, a single foreign policy, and a single military.

If Britain ultimately does choose to submerge itself into a fully united Europe, Americans will, of course, respect that choice. But until the choice is made, America should work hard to persuade Britain to choose otherwise—not to quit Europe, but to defend its military and political sovereignty *within* Europe. There are many ways in which we might influence that decision, but one of the most immediately attractive would be to offer British defense industries a better deal. Europe is trying to build a defense industry to rival North America's. The major European countries have agreed, for example, to build a new European fighter jet and a military transport aircraft, each country receiving a certain share of the work, each of them buying a certain number of planes. Britain has the largest defense procurement budget in Europe, so its participation is obviously essential to the success of the venture. And for many in the British defense industry, that participation is a more attractive proposition than attempting to sell into the American defense market, larded as it is with "buy American" provisions and restrictions on the transfer of technology even to allies as close as the United Kingdom. But it would be much *more* attractive to Britain if it could share on equal terms in the much larger U.S. defense procurement market instead. And why not? The United States has had a defense free trade agreement with Canada since 1958, and no important secrets seem to have been lost as a result. A U.S.-U.K.-Canada-Australia single market in defense production and procurement would 1) constitute a well-deserved reward to our closest friends, 2) improve combat efficiency by ensuring that we and our closest allies were using similar—ideally interoperable—equipment, while 3) reaffirming emphatically the benefits of close collaboration with the United States.

China

WITHOUT CHINESE AID, North Korea could never have sustained its ambitious nuclear program. That is why the United States has repeatedly appealed to Beijing for help in shutting down the program, thus far without success. It might seem that China would share our interest in denying nuclear weapons to Kim Jong Il. Not only is he an erratic and dangerous ruler, but he's an erratic and dangerous ruler who could easily start or provoke a war right next door to China. Yet China has done nothing of consequence to help solve the Korean problem, and despite the unrelenting optimism of our diplomats, Beijing seems unlikely to change its studied indifference anytime soon.

It is widely believed at the Department of State that the Chinese, who dislike and distrust Kim Jong Il, can be persuaded to help us this time around. They are almost certainly wrong. For while China does not wish its client-state actually to provoke a war on the peninsula, it is quite content that North Korea's blackmail policy should transfer the costs of supporting the North Korean regime from China's back onto ours—not to mention Japan's and South Korea's. As the Chinese, like Kim Jong Il himself, appear to regard the North Korean multipurpose bomb as a goose laying golden eggs, they are hardly likely to serve it up for our dinner.

Since the pragmatists in the Chinese Communist Party prevailed over the Maoist diehards in the mid-1970s, American policy makers have hoped that free trade, foreign investment, and economic growth would transform China into a reasonably open, stable, and peaceful society. Nor is it yet possible to dismiss those hopes as misplaced: It could yet be true that the people of China will seek to achieve their ambitions through peaceful trade, development, and progress. Richard Perle visited China in September 1976. By coincidence he was there when Mao Zedong died, and he remembers being introduced to Mao's immediate successor as general secretary of the Communist Party, Hua Guofeng. Hua, who smoked incessantly, paused to light a cigarette during a long monologue on China's role in the world. With a lighted match in one hand and a cigarette in the other, he asked whether we knew the Chinese word for "match." Then, as the match burned toward his fingers, he dramatically and slowly said, "The word for this match is made up of two ideograms. One means 'fire' and the other 'foreign.' Can you imagine the humiliation—that we, the inventors of gunpowder, should be reduced to calling this match 'foreign fire'?" Whatever hope we may have that China will move toward greater openness through a process of economic-leading-to-political reform, we will have to deal with a deep-seated Chinese determination that their great and ancient civilization should recover its place as a great power.

Because we hope that China may still evolve into a more

open society, it is important for the United States to support a policy of open trade with China, including permanent normal trade relations and China's entry into the World Trade Organization. If any one policy can drag China toward greater liberty, it is free trade, with its diffusion of wealth and power beyond the control of the government. In the meantime, the United States should make it clear to the Chinese that Americans want a sustainable, friendly relationship with China, provided that the Chinese respect American values and American interests in the world and in the region—including the freedom of Taiwan. While we cannot determine the ultimate relationship between Beijing and Taipei, we can—and must— insist that the relationship be settled peacefully.

The best way to deal with a country with which we have differences is to be clear and direct: "If you do *this,* we shall do *that.*" Not: "We might consider doing *that.*" Not: "We reserve the option of doing *that.*" But: "We *shall* do that."

That is why President Bush was right to reply, when asked in a television interview in April 2001 about a hypothetical Chinese invasion of Taiwan, that he would do "whatever it took to help Taiwan defend herself." These words stunned much of the foreign policy establishment, which had for more than twenty years urged a policy of "strategic ambiguity" on Taiwan. Some of the president's critics maliciously suggested that he had suffered a slip of the tongue. Not so. He was repeating, rather more bluntly, the very same point he had made at the Reagan Library in November 1999, in the most important foreign policy speech of his presidential campaign: "We do not deny there is one China. But we deny the right of Beijing to impose their rule on a free people. As I've said before, we will help Taiwan to defend itself."

For the foreseeable future, the U.S.-Chinese relationship will be a delicate one. The best way to ensure that nothing gets broken is to be direct. We and the Chinese can be friendly. But a friendly relationship will not be possible if China uses its growing economic and military power to intimidate or impose its will on our Asian friends and allies. And we will find it difficult to warm to the Chinese if they are not with us in our war on terrorism or if they continue to abuse the basic human rights of their citizens.

Our Asian policy should be clearly set out:

- A defense partnership with Japan, Australia, and other willing Asian democracies as intimate and enduring as the NATO alliance. The Japanese are already amending their laws to make possible closer defense collaboration with the United States, but they are still burdened by constitutional restrictions, arising out of World War II, on the establishment and operation of military forces. China should know that any attempt to bully any one of its democratic neighbors will be resisted by all of them—no ifs, buts, or exceptions.

- A credible military guarantee for Taiwan. President Bush's words must be backed by unambiguous actions: military-to-military contacts, ship visits by American vessels, and the sale of those advanced technologies most likely to deter Chinese military action, including submarines and antimissile technology. The Chinese will howl. Let them. Defensive weapons pose problems only for aggressors.

- A regional defense system against ballistic missiles, possibly based on naval platforms. This would go a long way toward neutralizing North Korea's nuclear arsenal.

- Greater South Korean responsibility for its own defense. Part of South Korea's capital city, Seoul, is within artillery range of these North Korean guns. There are highly capable counterbattery systems available that track incoming shells, compute their trajectory back to the point of origin, and return fire, all within seconds. You would think that the South Koreans would long ago have acquired and deployed them. But they have not. Unfortunately, *their* vulnerability adversely affects *our* security, since it raises the potential cost of military action. We should say to the South Koreans: We will continue to join in your defense, but only if you make a substantially larger effort to defend yourselves.

South Asia

SOUTH ASIA PRESENTS the United States with a hideous tangle of strategic, political, and ethical conundrums.

Take Pakistan, for example. Pakistan has become one of our most important allies in the war on terror. The Pakistanis helped us capture Khalid Shaikh Mohammed, the 9/11 mastermind. Without Pakistani support, our job in Afghanistan would have been far more difficult.

Yet at the same time, the Pakistani government and prominent individual Pakistanis have provided aid and comfort to our worst enemies. Pakistan gave the North Koreans nuclear technology in exchange for North Korean missile know-how, and this relationship continued well after 9/11. Pakistan has provided aid to the Iranian nuclear program as well. Pakistan allowed—and in some cases apparently assisted—high-placed members of the Taliban to escape American forces in December 2001.

Individual Pakistanis who earn their living selling nuclear know-how go about their business unmolested. A veteran of the Pakistani nuclear program, Sultan Bashiruddin Mahmoud, traveled to Afghanistan in 1999–2000 and was solicited by Osama bin Laden. Mahmoud has been put under house arrest and questioned intensely, but one question that we would like to have answered is, Why were there so many Islamic extremists in the Pakistani nuclear program in the first place? "There are lots of them over there," a nonextremist Pakistani scientist told *The Washington Post,* referring to Pakistan's nuclear-research facilities. "In recent years it's become a quite frightening place to go to. You see all these long beards."*

Pakistan has a record of using terrorism as a weapon

---

* Peter Baker, "Pakistani Scientist Who Met bin Laden Failed Polygraphs, Renewing Suspicions," *The Washington Post,* March 3, 2002, p. A1.

against India in the dispute over Kashmir, and many people suspect that elements in the Pakistani secret service continue to support Kashmiri extremism to this day.

Probably the single most alarming fact about Pakistan is the fragile political basis of its current pro-American policy. In more than half a century since independence, Pakistan has scarcely once known a peaceful and legal transfer of power. The current leader, Pervez Musharraf, himself seized power in a military coup. Control of the Pakistani state is perpetually up for grabs—and with it comes control of Pakistan's stockpile of nuclear warheads.

President Musharraf has proven himself to be an able and realistic leader who has successively jettisoned the Taliban, avoided war with India, and curtailed the Kashmiri terrorists. But will he last? And who will succeed him? Pakistan is a troubled society. Its economy is still dominated by feudal landlords. Corrupt politicians enrich themselves at the expense of a poor and growing population. Foreign investors shun the place. Its people (along with those of the former East Pakistan, Bangladesh) remain the least literate in the region. Without hope or opportunity, many Pakistanis have turned to religion for comfort—and the religion propounded to them is increasingly radical and hate-filled.

Impoverished Pakistan has become a favored destination for Saudi Arabia's poisonous philanthropy. Saudi-funded religious schools drill boys to memorize the Koran in its original Arabic, a language few of them will ever understand. They learn no trade or skills, no math, no science, no Western language—only deadening rituals and murderous prejudice. If they fail to recite correctly the texts they must learn by rote, they are beaten. They are allowed no contact with women. By the time they "graduate," they are unemployable, deformed personalities. Meanwhile, in city slums and unelectrified villages, Saudi-funded imams preach jealousy and rage to populations baffled by their country's backward slide and repeated military defeats.

Some months ago, Richard Perle participated in a BBC broadcast that linked together studio audiences in New York, London, and Karachi. Every one of the Pakistani participants—a diplomat, an engineer, a university professor, a popular journalist—denounced the United States. Some suggested that 9/11 was an Israeli plot, another that Osama bin Laden was innocent of any wrongdoing, and a third that the United States "deserved" what it got on 9/11. If these are the ideas and sentiments of middle-class Pakistanis, we have good reason to pray for Pervez Musharraf—and to worry about his country.

The Pakistani military is usually thought to be immune to these Islamic trends. Pakistani officers almost caricature the British military tradition, with their clipped mustaches, short pants, swagger sticks, and Sandhurst vocabulary. (Pakistani colonels must be the only people on earth who still use the expression *old boy*.) But unlike Turkey, Pakistan is not a secular state; it was founded, instead, explicitly as a sectarian Muslim nation. Nor is the Pakistani military immune to the allure of Arab cash. Men of Musharraf's generation were already mature by the time Saudi money began to infiltrate Pakistan. They seem to have been able to accept it without being unduly influenced by it. The next generation may have other ideas—and bombs that are today Islamic in name only may someday end up as weapons of jihad.

More than one-third of the world's 1 billion Muslims live in the Indian subcontinent: 150 million of them in Pakistan, another 140 million in Bangladesh, 100 million in India itself. These subcontinental Muslims are inheritors of a religious tradition as different as can be from the primitive doctrines of the Wahhabis. Nearly two hundred years before the American Founders inscribed religious liberty into the U.S. Constitution, an Indian Muslim named Akbar was ruling a multireligious, multiethnic empire on the subcontinent with the motto "All faiths deserve reverence. By thus acting, a man exalts his own faith and at the same time serves humanity."

America does not have the power to persuade subcontinental Muslims to choose tolerance and compassion over hate and jihad. But we can do our part to rescue the subcontinent's people from the poverty and conflict that have made them so receptive to fanatical versions of Islam. Nobody appreciates the importance of military power in the war on terrorism more than the authors of this book. But South Asia is one place where nonmilitary power can do the most good. We must help Pakistan modernize and reform—and we must do what we can to dispel the animosities and jealousies that keep Pakistan and India on the verge of war. Above all, we must liberate and protect Pakistan from the malign influence of Saudi missionaries.

To those ends, we should

- Accept the subcontinent's nuclear weapons as an unwelcome but unalterable fact and drop all remaining sanctions against India and Pakistan. The sanctions were ill conceived from the beginning. There was never the slightest chance they would succeed in halting either the Pakistani or Indian nuclear program. Their only effect was to estrange the United States from both countries.

- Broaden our direct military-to-military relationships with Pakistan and India and also Bangladesh and Sri Lanka, to encourage the promotion of Western-oriented officers, to teach effective and humane counterterrorism tactics, and to introduce reliable controls to prevent nuclear weapons from falling into unauthorized hands.

- Increase U.S. aid to the subcontinent and focus the money on providing a more appealing education than the local Islamic colleges offer. In chapter 6, we talked about the specific importance of girls' education, but we must offer help to boys as well. We should even support Islamic schools, provided they offer equal educational opportunities to both sexes; teach marketable skills; instruct in the local language or in some other modern language, instead of ancient Arabic; and refrain from racial, ethnic, or nationalistic incitement.

- Promote peace by promoting subcontinental economic integration. In chapter 6, we talked about the importance of lowering first world trade barriers to third world goods and services. We should offer not only Pakistan but also Bangladesh, Sri Lanka, and India an even better deal: a comprehensive free trade agreement with the United States—*provided they sign the same agreement with one another.* Unrestricted access to our markets should not be a reward for the mixed record of the past; it should be a lever to alter the future. If the Pakistanis want to sell us towels unhindered, they should drop their own barriers to trade with India. When Pakistan and India become each other's largest customers, neither country will be quite so quick on the nuclear trigger; when Indian rice feeds Bangladesh's poor, the Bangladeshis will not listen so raptly to preachers of anti-Indian jihad. Trade does not always bring peace. But protectionism seeds war.

Russia

RUSSIA HAS PLAYED a double game from the very beginning of the war on terror. In Afghanistan, President Vladimir Putin chose to be helpful: Russia supported the United States at the United Nations and acquiesced as American troops were deployed into former Soviet republics like Uzbekistan. Yet at the very same time the Russians sold crucial nuclear material to Iran and joined France to protect Iraq.

Some might describe this two-faced policy as ambiguous. We think it is very clear. President Putin could have chosen to act as a consistent friend of the United States. He did not do so. He has instead conveyed a message that his friendship is available, but at a price—and that same friendship will be sold to someone else when Putin can get a higher price.

The government of Iran has placed billions of dollars' worth of orders with Russian arms manufacturers. More than money, however, is at stake. These Iranian projects keep alive the Russian armaments industry, an industry that faced extinction when Russian military spending collapsed in the 1990s—but that Putin seems determined to nurture for the larger future he seems to envision for Russia.

Since 1990, the United States has labored mightily to integrate Russia into the Western world. Money, technical assistance, trade and financial agreements: Whatever Russia seemed to need, we willingly offered. We even suppressed our own moral qualms to soothe Russian sensibilities, hushing our criticism of Russia's two Chechen wars. As many as 150,000 people may have died violently in Chechnya since 1991; 200,000 Chechens have been made refugees. The second Chechen war was provoked when four apartment buildings in two Russian cities were bombed in September 1999, killing more than 300 civilians. The Russian government blamed Chechen Islamic terrorists—a story that did not seem very convincing even at the time and that became a whole lot less convincing after a team of Russian secret policemen were caught shortly afterward planting a large bomb in the basement of an apartment building in Ryazan. (Their story: They were testing "security measures.")

The United States should seek the warmest possible relationship with Russia. But Russia is not Germany in 1945—a defeated enemy we can remake at will. It is much more like Germany in 1918—a defeated enemy that has adopted a democratic constitution, but where many of the most sinister figures from the old regime still retain considerable power. The Russian army is the Soviet army, only smaller. The FSB is the KGB under a new name. And Vladimir Putin . . . well, we still don't fully know who he is.

What we do know is this: Our relationship with Russia is not an alliance, not even a friendship, but rather a series of transactions. In these transactions, it is imperative that we do not allow ourselves to be cheated. We should disabuse the Russians of the illusion that they can sell deadly weapons to our enemies and preserve any kind of relationship with us. One symbolic blow that would sting a great deal: Although the Russian economy is now roughly the size of that of the Netherlands, Russia has out of courtesy been invited to the annual summit meetings of the seven major industrial powers since 1997. We should not be wasting such compliments upon the salesmen of the Iranian bomb.

Russia has likewise been allowed to take part in NATO summits—an invitation that Russia earned in the days when it aspired to be a kind of ally of the West's. If Russia opts instead to arm and equip those who would destroy the West, it is hard to see why these invitations should continue either.

Nor should we keep silent any longer about the atrocities

in Chechnya in order to buy some temporary Russian assistance on some security problem. Whatever other business we transact with our unreliable Russian partners, America's principles ought never to be put up for sale.

The United Nations

IT MIGHT SEEM odd to end a survey like this with a section on the United Nations. As Americans see it, the UN is not a force in itself, but merely an international forum in which the countries that *are* forces can express themselves.

But for many of our friends, the UN has taken on a reality of its own. For them, the UN is more than a mere convention of governments, some democratic, most not; some important, most not. For many idealistic people in Britain and Australia, the Netherlands and Singapore, Mexico and South Africa, the UN is exactly what it pretends to be: the parliament of the world.

When it suits them, many American liberals profess to feel the same way, and the winter of 2002–2003 was one of those times when it did suit them. Congress had voted to authorize the use of force in Iraq in October 2002; in November 2002, the United Nations Security Council approved Resolution 1441, which threatened Iraq with "serious consequences" if it did not fully explain the current whereabouts of the weapons of mass destruction it had previously itself confessed to possessing. Many Americans, including many senior Democratic members of Congress, argued that all this authority was not enough: They demanded President Bush should return to the UN for one resolution more.

There were any number of good retorts to this demand. The Security Council had adopted more than a dozen resolutions since 1990 ordering Iraq to disarm—why would one more constitute a magic number? Nobody had suggested that President Clinton needed to return to the UN for more authority when he waged aerial war against Iraq back in 1998. Anyway, since when did the United States require the Security Council's permission to defend itself? As foreign affairs commentator Charles Krauthammer kept wondering, If the war was necessary, how would the disapproval of Chile and Cameroon make it unnecessary? And if the war was unnecessary, how could their approval make it necessary?

But a democratic world is governed by opinion as much as by law. And in the opinion of a great many people around the world, a Security Council resolution has talismanic power. The United States itself has acknowledged that power many times since 1990. We asked the Security Council for permission to fight Iraq in 1991. We asked permission again in 1998 to deal with Serbia's campaign of atrocities in Kosovo. We asked permission to invade Afghanistan, and in the end the Bush administration did twice ask permission to overthrow Saddam.

Now, in the minds of many Americans, these requests were perfunctory courtesies, like saying "Excuse me" before you push your way onto a crowded subway car: You'd still board the car whether the other riders excused you or not.

Unsurprisingly, however, this selective attitude to the UN irritates UN enthusiasts in other countries. As they see it, when we ask the UN for permission, we accept the UN's authority—and we then ought to be bound by the UN's decisions. If we salute the UN when it supports us and disregard it when it does not, we open ourselves to the accusation that we are hypocrites and scofflaws.

Of course, the world is full of hypocrites and scofflaws. Few governments in the world, for example, praise human rights more ardently than does the government of France, and few have a worse record of supporting tyrants and killers, from Emperor Bokassa I of the Central African Republic through the genocidal Hutu leadership in Rwanda to Saddam Hussein himself. France ardently supports the prerogatives of the Security Council because, of course, France has a veto there. In a world without the UN, it would be obvious to all that the opinions and desires of the president of France mattered a great deal less than those of, say, the prime minister of India. But the United States is a very different kind of country from France. Our claims to world leadership rest not just on our power and wealth but on our moral authority. If we say one thing and do another, if we appear to uphold our principles only when they serve our immediate interests, then our actions give credibility to our enemies when they call us a rogue nation, an imperial state, and a threat to world order.

Our words and deeds must be aligned, and the United Nations system as now constituted makes it impossible to align them. Here's why: The United Nations was created at a time when the great threat to world peace was an invasion across the borders of one country by the army of another. For that reason, Article 51 of the UN Charter recognizes an "inherent" right of self-defense against "armed attack." But under the UN Charter, anything less than an "armed attack" is a mere dispute, which the parties must refer to the Security Council for adjudication. It is not an "armed attack" against the United States when Syria sends money and weapons to Hezbollah, although Hezbollah has attacked Americans in the past and will almost certainly do so in the future. Nor is it an "armed attack" on the United States if Pakistan shares its nuclear technology with North Korea, although a North Korean nuclear bomb would constitute an extremely grave threat to the United States. Nor yet is it an "armed attack" for Iran to grant refuge to al-Qaeda terrorists, although al-Qaeda is daily plotting to murder Americans by the thousands.

These are acts of aggression just as surely as sending warships to shell our ports, but the UN Charter does not recognize them as such. It is stuck in the era of blitzkriegs and manned bombers—even as modern aggressors resort to covert operations, cyberwarfare, assassinations, and state-sponsored terrorism.

The UN is not an entirely useless organization. Some of its agencies do some good work, possibly almost enough to offset the corruption of all the other agencies. It creates employment for the less employable relatives of presidents for life. It gives smaller countries a feeling that their views count. And when the chamber is empty and touring schoolchildren walk the halls, the extravagant building can for a quiet moment seem to give substance to the age-old dream of a world without war.

But the UN also does considerable harm. Its resolutions force countries to take stands on issues they might otherwise have sidestepped. How was it in Chile's interest, for example, to vote against the U.S.-sponsored resolution on Iraq at the very same time that it was completing a free trade agreement with the United States? By bad luck, however, 2002–2003 was Chile's year to occupy one of the temporary seats on the Security Council—and domestic political pressures obliged Chile's leaders to cast a pointlessly self-damaging negative.

The UN regularly turns itself into the stage for a hackneyed political melodrama, where bored crowds watch endless replays of the same dreary performance, dully booing the never changing villains (Israel, the United States), spiritlessly applauding the stereotyped heroes (Cuba, Zimbabwe, the Palestinian Authority). When the stage lights switch off, the crowd rushes for the exits, knowing full well that in real life the villains are not at all villainous and the heroes are thieves, thugs, liars, and killers. The UN regularly broadcasts a spectacle as dishonest and morally deadening as a Stalinist show trial, a televised ritual of condemnation that inflames hatreds and sustains quarrels that might otherwise fade away.

The UN seldom addresses the United States with the naked hostility it exhibits toward its smaller victims. But precisely because we have endorsed its pretensions in the past, we suffer more from the UN's defects than even the Israelis do. It hurt us to appeal to the UN for that second Iraq resolution and then fail to get it. It will hurt us if we seek UN help on North Korea or Iran, are defeated by a Chinese or Russian or French veto, and then proceed all the same.

So, a suggestion: Before bringing any new security issue to the UN, we should make it our first business to demand a revision of the UN's rules in such a way as to restore the UN's relevance—and to enhance our own security. The UN must commit itself to the proposition that harboring, supporting, or financing terrorists in itself constitutes an Article 51 act of aggression against the country those terrorists target. This can be done by amending the UN Charter—or, alternatively, through an interpretive resolution of the Security Council or by some other means altogether. Whatever the method, the UN must endorse our "inherent" right to defend ourselves against new threats just as forcefully as we are entitled to defend ourselves against old threats. If not, we should formally reject the UN's authority over our war on terror.

Americans will never hesitate to present our case to the world, to answer questions, and to rebut false charges. And it may be for some time to come that the UN is the most convenient forum in which to engage in public debate before a global audience. But if the UN cannot or will not revise its rules in ways that establish beyond question the legality of the measures the United States must take to protect the American people, then we should unashamedly and explicitly reject the jurisdiction of these rules.

The UN is not some immemorial achievement of the human race. It was created within living memory by men and women no cleverer than those alive today to respond to the dangers and necessities of a particular time. Times change. Dangers change. Necessities change. Institutions should change, too. And if institutions like the UN cannot change, that is not an indictment of us. It is an indictment of them—and reason enough for them to be discarded.

THESE ARE OUR realities. We might wish they were easier or more favorable—but we have faced darker realities before and overcome them. Nor will we ever give up trying to improve those realities: to soothe jealousies, assuage doubts, and win friends. The terrorists who threaten us threaten the whole civilized world; there is hardly any country anywhere that will not be more secure if we win—and far less secure if we lose.

We should never be too proud to appeal for help and to be grateful when we receive it—but we should not make the mistake of relying on it. The temptations to others to lie low and leave the difficulties of war to us will always be strong. The war on terror will be a war of shifting coalitions. Our allies in Iraq were not the same as our allies in Afghanistan, and our allies in future campaigns may differ again. We do not have to like this fact, but we must not be daunted by it. We cannot permit the weaknesses of others to govern us. We are the terrorists' first target, so this war is first and foremost our war. We are fighting on behalf of the civilized world. We will never cease to hope for the civilized world's support. But if it is lacking, as it may be, then we have to say, like the gallant lonely British soldier in David Low's famous cartoon of 1940: "Very well, alone."

9. A WAR FOR LIBERTY

We exhibit to mankind the remarkable spectacle of a people attacked by unprovoked enemies, without any imputation or even suspicion of offence. . . . In our own native land, in defence of the freedom that is our birthright, and which we ever enjoyed till the late violation of it: for the protection of our property, acquired solely by the honest industry of our forefathers and ourselves, against violence actually offered, we have taken up arms. We shall lay them down when hostilities shall cease on the part of the aggressors, and all danger of their being renewed shall be removed, and not before.
—THOMAS JEFFERSON, "Declaration of the Causes and Necessity of Taking Up Arms," July 6, 1775

FOR TWO HUNDRED years, tyrannical rulers have dreaded America's influence over their subjugated peoples. As long as the United States has existed, that existence has demonstrated that freedom is possible. As long as the United States has prospered, our prosperity has shown that freedom is rewarded. And now that the United States has become the greatest of all great powers in world history, its triumph has shown that freedom is irresistible.

If you are an Iranian mullah clutching on to billions in stolen oil wealth, or a Saudi imam terrified of the loss of your congregants, or a Palestinian would-be dictator rallying your people to suicide instead of trade and cooperation—the excitement and appeal of American life is your deadliest enemy.

"We want to be like America," one Iraqi man excitedly told the brigadier of the 101st Airborne just days after the liberation of Baghdad.*

"We want to be like America," a group of Afghan refugees burbled as they returned to their former homes after the overthrow of the Taliban.†

"We want to be like America," say the student protesters in Teheran.

And as long as the Islamic extremists' subjects repeat such things, for so long will the United States be militant Islam's target. If ever there were a war of self-defense, the war on terror is that war.

This is a scenario for a long war, but it is not a scenario for endless war. No lie lasts forever, and militant Islam is a lie. It proposes to restore the vanished glory of a great civilization through crimes that horrify the conscience of the world. It invokes the language of liberation—but it intends to fasten unthinking, unquestioning slavery on the minds of the people of

---

* Kimberly Hefling, "A Snap Election, Pleas for Help as Iraqis Meet with U.S. Troops," Associated Press Worldstream, April 19, 2003.

† Mort Rosbenblum, "Afghan Minorities, Who Could Add Up to a Majority, Want Their Country Back from the Taliban," Associated Press Worldstream, October 17, 2001.

one-fifth of the world. It claims the authority of God for its own cruelty and evil.

The United States has been reproached even by many who should know better for inserting itself into Iraq rather than letting the Iraqis rule themselves. But it is only because we did insert ourselves into Iraq that the Iraqis have any hope of ruling themselves—and the same will be true in Iran and everywhere else in the Islamic world where we must fight.

Kofi Annan complained in July 2003 that democracy cannot be imposed by force. Really? Men from Annan's Ghana fought and died in the Burmese jungles to defeat the Japanese army—and thereby to impose democracy by force on Japan. Democracy seems to have made quite a success of itself there, too.

We do not show our respect for human difference by shrugging indifferently when people somehow different from ourselves are brutalized in body and spirit. If a foreign people lack liberty, it is not because of some misguided act of cultural choice. It is because they have been seized and oppressed and tyrannized. To say that we are engaged in "imposing American values" when we liberate people is to imply that there are peoples on this earth who value their own subjugation.

It is the terrorists, rather, who intend to impose *their* values, upon Muslims and non-Muslims alike. They inflict misery and death upon Muslims—but promise to compensate by inflicting still greater misery and death upon non-Muslims. The terrorists espouse an ideology of conquest, just as the Nazis and the Soviets did; and as we defeated the Nazis and communists by championing freedom not only for ourselves but also for Germans and Russians, so we must now do the same for the Islamic people who are both terrorism's prime constituency and its principal victims.

Annan is wrong. Much more often than not, democracy will not have a chance *unless* it is aided from outside—and by force if necessary. As those Iraqis, Afghans, and Iranians told us, people all over the world want the benefits of American democracy—but they do not always possess the skills to launch a representative government by only their unaided strength. We can help, as we helped in Western Europe and Japan. Democracy is most apt to survive and flourish when the local economy is strong—and creating the conditions for a successful economy can again require outside help, like the help we provided when we encouraged the democratization of Central America in the 1980s. Sometimes a small democracy is threatened by powerful external enemies—and the United States has historically always stood ready to protect small free countries against powerful unfree neighbors, as we now stand ready to protect Taiwan against China.

To call this "empire" as do some opponents of the war—and some rash supporters, too—is to wrong ourselves. To call it "empire" belittles the many small countries that have turned to the United States for protection, rightly confident that our assistance would not impair their independence and sovereignty. The American record on this score is not perfect. But it is a record to be proud of all the same.

We mentioned before the strange feeling of the UN headquarters on a quiet weekend afternoon. A visitor can sink into one of the quaint futuristic chairs in the corridors, close his or her eyes, and dream for a minute the dream that built the place. The authors of this book are not immune to that dream—even as we recognize that the UN has traduced and betrayed it. A world at peace; a world governed by law; a world in which all peoples are free to find their own destinies: That dream has not yet come true, it will not come true soon, but if it ever does come true, it will be brought into being by American armed might and defended by American might, too. America's vocation is not an imperial vocation. Our vocation is to support justice with power. It is a vocation that has earned us terrible enemies. It is a vocation that has made us, at our best moments, the hope of the world.

APPENDIX

Current List of Designated Foreign Terrorist Organizations
(as of May 23, 2003)

1. Abu Nidal Organization (ANO)—Iraq/Lebanon
2. Abu Sayyaf Group—Philippines
3. Al-Aqsa Martyrs Brigade—West Bank (Palestinians)
4. Armed Islamic Group (GIA)—Algeria
5. 'Asbat al-Ansar—Lebanon
6. Aum Shinrikyo—Japan
7. Basque Fatherland and Liberty (ETA)
8. Communist Party of the Philippines/New People's Army (CPP/NPA)
9. Al-Gama'a al-Islamiyya (Islamic Group)—Egypt
10. Hamas (Islamic Resistance Movement)
11. Harakat ul-Mujahidin (HUM)—Kashmir
12. Hezbollah (Party of God)
13. Islamic Movement of Uzbekistan (IMU)
14. Jaish-e-Mohammed (JEM) (Army of Mohammed)—Pakistan
15. Jemaah Islamiya (JI)—Indonesia, Malaysia, southern Philippines
16. Al-Jihad (Egyptian Islamic Jihad)

17. Kahane Chai (Kach)—Israel
18. Kurdistan Workers' Party (PKK) aka Kurdistan Freedom and Democracy Congress (KADEK)
19. Lashkar-e-Jhangvi—Pakistan
20. Lashkar-e-Tayyiba (LT) (Army of the Righteous)—Pakistan
21. Liberation Tigers of Tamil Eelam (LTTE)—Sri Lanka
22. Mujahedin-e Khalq Organization (MEK)—Iran, Iraq
23. National Liberation Army (ELN)—Columbia
24. Palestine Islamic Jihad (PIJ)
25. Palestine Liberation Front (PLF)
26. Popular Front for the Liberation of Palestine (PFLP)
27. PFLP—General Command (PFLPGC)
28. al-Qaeda
29. Real IRA
30. Revolutionary Armed Forces of Colombia (FARC)
31. Revolutionary Nuclei (formerly ELA)—Greece
32. Revolutionary Organization 17 November—Greece
33. Revolutionary People's Liberation Army/Front (DHKP/C)—Turkey
34. Salafist Group for Call and Combat (GSPC)—Algeria
35. Shining Path (Sendero Luminoso, SL)—Peru
36. United Self-Defense Forces of Colombia (AUC)

ACKNOWLEDGMENTS

THIS BOOK WAS born in the fertile mind of David Gerson, executive vice president of the American Enterprise Institute. Gerson pointed out that we had been talking together for a decade—and that after all those spoken words, maybe we ought to write some of them down. For that brain wave and so much else besides, we owe him thanks.

We owe equal thanks to Christopher DeMuth, AEI's president: one of those rare people who manage to combine a good heart and shrewd intellect in exactly the right proportion. His kindness and support were essential to this project—and to just about everything else that American conservatives (neo and *ancienne*) have accomplished over the past two decades.

Our researcher, Andrew Kelly, answered impossible questions with meticulous care at incredible speed. Daniel Feith found facts in real time. Murray Frum, Brian Lapping, Laurie Mylroie, Harold Rhode, Michael Rubin, and Peter Worthington generously sacrificed their time to read and comment on some or all of the manuscript. Michael Ledeen also read the manuscript and, through his own important work, helped us understand the terror masters. We thank them for their wisdom and advice. The final responsibility for the words herein is, of course, our own.

Jonathan Karp was the cleverest, bravest, and wisest of editors. Jennifer Rudolph Walsh had the unenviable task of representing both coauthors—and did the job with all her usual force and imagination. And Sona Vogel and Steve Messina faultlessly copyedited the manuscript under the most trying of circumstances.

David Frum is particularly grateful to Richard Lowry, Jay Nordlinger, and William F. Buckley for allowing him to develop and sharpen his thoughts in *National Review* and *National Review Online;* and to Peter and Yvonne Worthington for their never-failing (and this time extra-lengthy!) hospitality on the shores of Lake Ontario.

All books impose heavy involuntary sacrifices on the families of their authors. This book—written at high speed through high summer—was more onerous than most. So a special thanks, seasoned with apologies, to Miranda, Nathaniel, and Beatrice Frum, and to Jonathan Perle. Every page here was inspired by the same thought: How can we leave you a better and safer world?

Each of us has said our own thanks in our own way to our wives, Leslie Barr and Danielle Crittenden Frum. But there is perhaps one more thing to be said here, in Browning's words:

> My own, confirm me! If I tread
> This path back, is it not in pride
> To think how little I dreamed it led
> To an age so blest that, by its side,
> Youth seems the waste instead?

ABOUT THE AUTHORS

DAVID FRUM, a former special assistant to President George W. Bush, is a resident fellow at the American Enterprise Institute and a contributing editor of *National Review*.

RICHARD PERLE served as an assistant secretary of defense in the Reagan administration and as chairman of the Defense Policy Board under President George W. Bush. He is a resident fellow at the American Enterprise Institute.

ABOUT THE TYPE

This book was set in Sabon, a typeface designed by the well-known German typographer Jan Tschichold (1902–74). Sabon's design is based upon the original letter forms of Claude Garamond and was created specifically to be used for three sources: foundry type for hand composition, Linotype, and Monotype. Tschichold named his typeface for the famous Frankfurt typefounder Jacques Sabon, who died in 1580.